THE WORLD OF SCIENCE
ASTRONOMY

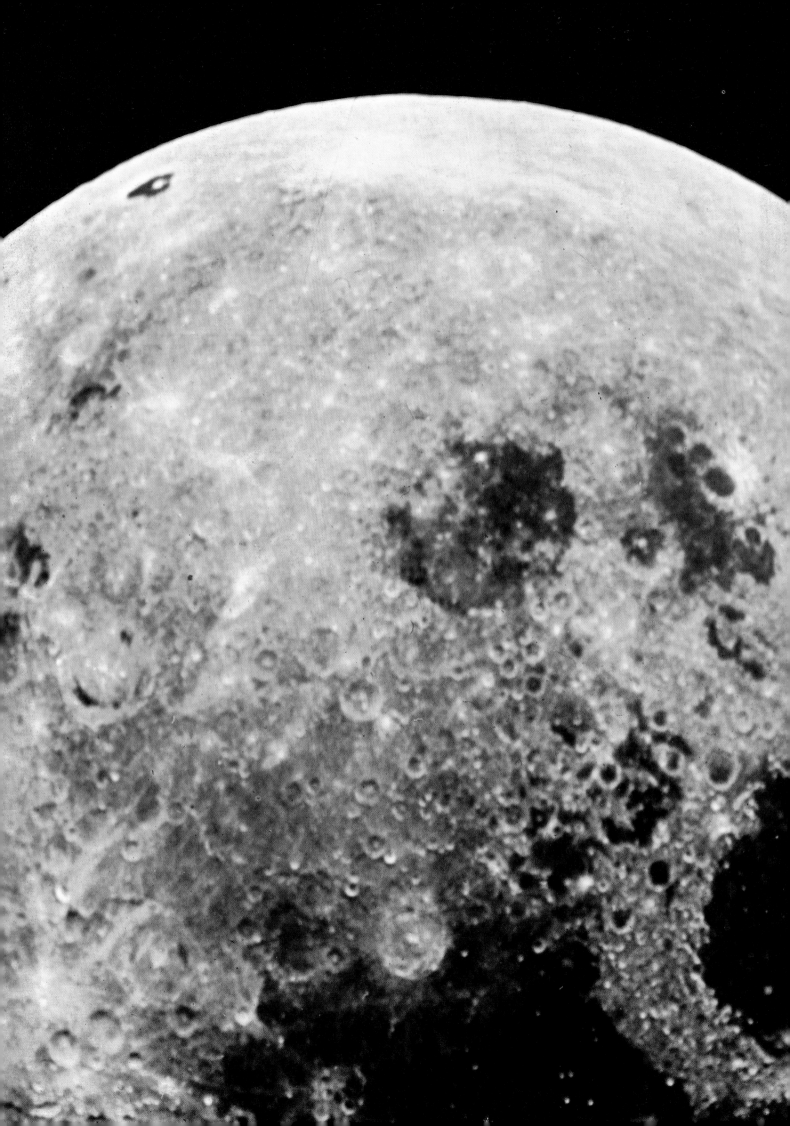

THE WORLD OF SCIENCE
ASTRONOMY

PETER LANCASTER BROWN

Facts On File Publications
New York, New York ● Bicester, England

ASTRONOMY

Copyright © 1984 by Orbis Publishing Limited,
London

First published in the United States of America in
1984 by Facts on File, Inc., 460 Park Avenue South,
New York, N.Y.10016

First published in Great Britain in 1984 by Orbis
Publishing Limited, London

**Library of Congress Cataloging in Publication
Data**

Main entry under title:

The world of science.

  Includes index.
  Summary: A twenty-five volume encyclopedia of
scientific subjects, designed for eight- to twelve-year-
olds. One volume is entirely devoted to projects.
  1. Science—Dictionaries, Juvenile.   1. Science—
Dictionaries
Q121.J86   1984   500   84-1654

ISBN: 0-87196-985-8

Printed in Yugoslavia
10 9 8 7 6 5 4 3 2 1

Jacket photo courtesy of
T. Tracy/Image Bank

Previous pages The
Moon's surface
photographed during
the Apollo 8 lunar
orbit.

Editor Penny Clarke
Designer Roger Kohn

CONTENTS

◄The mass in the centre of this picture is one of the many gigantic clouds of gas and dust in the universe. It is 6,000 light years away from Earth and astronomers believe that new stars are forming within it.

Note There are some unusual words in this book. They are explained in the Glossary on page 62. The first time each word is used in the text it is printed in *italics*.

INTRODUCTION

EARLY SKY-WATCHERS

Long ago the Greeks called astronomy 'the Queen of Sciences'. It is certainly the oldest. But even before it became a real science, all ancient people were fascinated by what they saw in the sky. The Sun and the Moon became the gods of the day and the night. Soon people realised it was possible to use the Sun, Moon and even the stars to measure the passage of time by their regular 'clockwork' shifts round the sky.

►The Egyptian sky goddess Nut painted on a coffin lid with the boats of the Sun and the Moon and the twelve Zodiacal constellations along which the boats travelled in the heavens.

The Egyptians and Babylonians
By the time the Egyptians built their stone pyramids, around 2600 BC, and the Babylonians their mud-brick ziggurats a few hundred years earlier, they had measured the lengths of the seasons using the Sun and the stars. The Egyptians had also discovered that by carefully watching the dawn sky for the rise of the bright star Sirius they could predict when the annual flooding of the river Nile would occur, as this was the most important event in their agricultural calendar.

By this time, too, the Egyptians had become expert surveyors and were able to use the stars in the constellation of the Great Bear (Ursa Major) to point the four sides of the Great Pyramid *exactly* north, south, east and west.

The Egyptians called the Sun, Re. Because his heat and light brought life to the land, he became their most important god. When the mighty Re rose at dawn each day, they believed he voyaged across the sky in a boat over the back of the sky goddess whom they called Nut. Then at sunset, when the Sun dipped below the horizon, they thought he continued through the dark underworld. During the night the temple priests, fearful Re would sail away for ever, prayed for his return. Then at sunrise, when he answered their prayers, they sang hymns in his praise. The Egyptians believed the Moon was another god in a boat voyaging over Nut's back. We can see evidence for these old ideas, and even boats for stars, in carvings on temples and monuments and as paintings on the coffins of mummies in museums.

►The building of the great Egyptian pyramid at Giza in about 2600 BC was supervised by skilled astronomer-priests who used the stars of the Great Bear to make sure it faced *exactly* north. North was the most important direction as this faced the region of Dat (heaven) where the ancient Egyptians believed they would travel after death.

▼The astronomer-priests of Egypt had the Sphinx built to guard the great pyramids. Between the paws of this mythical creature is a shrine to the sun god.

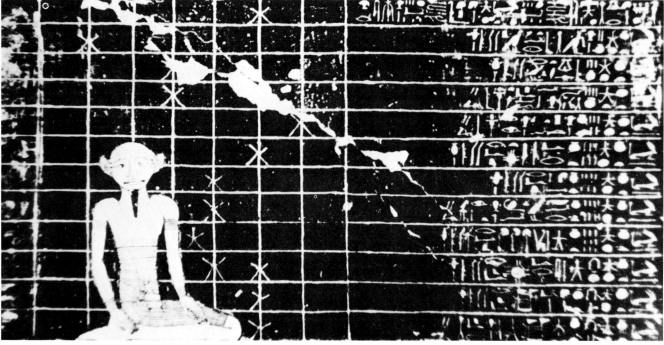

▲The ancient Egyptians used stars for telling the time of night. This picture shows a surviving star clock from the tomb of Rameses VII.

►Stonehenge near Salisbury Plain, England, was used as a calendar device by the Stone-Age Britons about 2500–1500 BC. It may also have been used to forecast eclipses of the Moon.

Stonehenge

The Egyptians and the Babylonians were not the only people to make use of the Sun and Moon. In southern Britain, between 2500 and 1500 BC, the Stone-Age astronomer-priests built the 'observatory' at Stonehenge to operate as a celestial calendar and also perhaps, in a more advanced way, as a kind of computer to predict when eclipses might occur.

Scientific astronomy begins

It is not until late Babylonian and early Greek times (700–300 BC) that we find written records which show a truly scientific approach to astronomy and how the ancient sky-watchers actually calculated events like eclipses. It was the Greek scholars who used earlier Egyptian and Babylonian ideas to organise astronomy as a proper science. The name astronomy comes from the Greek *astron*, meaning 'star', and *nomos*, meaning 'law'. From the Babylonians we have inherited the counting system based on sixty (sexagesimal), for example, the hour which is divided into 60 minutes. From the Egyptians we have inherited the system of a 24-hour day.

The Greek scholar Aristarchus of Samos (310–230 BC) was the first person to suggest that the Earth travelled round the Sun. Other Greek scholars, however, rejected this idea and still believed in an earlier Babylonian idea that it was the Sun and the starry heavens which revolved round the Earth (which they *appear* to do). Later another Greek scholar, Claudius Ptolemy (AD 120–180), living in Egypt, adopted the same Babylonian idea. He drew up a very complicated plan, known as the Ptolemaic system, to explain how all the heavenly bodies revolved round the Earth.

The Copernican system

Unfortunately Ptolemy was the most influential astronomer of his day and for a very long time after. Thirteen hundred years passed before the Polish astronomer Nicolaus Copernicus (1473–1543) challenged the Ptolemaic system. He went back to the old ideas of Aristarchus and wrote a book saying that the Earth and the other planets went round the Sun. Even so, some astronomers refused to accept the new Copernican system. One was the great Danish astronomer Tycho Brahe (1546–1601), often simply called Tycho. Tycho lived before the telescope was invented and died believing that the Ptolemaic theory was the correct one. Yet it was Tycho's own observations of the planet Mars, carefully made over many years from his famous observatory on the island of Hven in Denmark, which were later to prove beyond doubt that the Copernican system was the correct one.

◄Nicolaus Copernicus was a church official as well as a great astronomer. Because his theory that the Earth and all the other planets went round the Sun was quite revolutionary and contrary to the Church's teaching, he did not publish his work until nearly at the end of his life.

▲An old print showing Tycho Brahe, the Danish astronomer, at work in his observatory. Although he lived and worked after Copernicus' death, he did not share his views. Like Ptolemy, Tycho believed that the Earth was the centre of the Universe. But it was Tycho's work that proved Copernicus was right.

The Sun's family

The earliest sky-watchers soon noticed that certain bright 'stars' were not fixed in the night sky but shifted, or wandered, in relation to others. These later became known as planets from the Greek word *planetes*, meaning 'to wander'.

The earliest sky-watchers also noticed there were five bright wanderers, or planets. During Greek and Roman times they became known as Mercury, Venus, Mars, Jupiter and Saturn – all names derived from mythological persons invented in the ancient world. The other planets we know today, also named after mythological persons, were discovered after the invention of the telescope in 1608. Uranus was found in 1781, Neptune in 1846, Pluto in 1930 and Chiron, a small planet lying between Saturn and Uranus, in 1977.

As well as these major planets there are a large number of minor planets, or asteroids. The first of these, Ceres, was discovered with the telescope in 1801. Other members of the Sun's family include our own Moon, the moons, or satellites, of other planets and comets, meteors, fireballs and meteorites.

All the family members revolve round the Sun at varying distances in paths called orbits. The orbits, like those of the major planets, are almost circular in shape, but the orbits of comets and asteroids are often egg-shaped, or elliptical

Sol, our local star

You may sometimes read or hear about 'the star called Sol', but this is just another name for the Sun to emphasise it is a star like those others we see twinkling in the night sky. The main difference between a planet like our own Earth and an average star like Sol is that planets are cold bodies while stars are usually very hot and are made up of gas in violent agitation.

A typical star like Sol resembles a continuously exploding hydrogen bomb or a power station operating on a vast scale. It shines with the light produced in its nuclear furnace deep inside. Because of this astronomers refer to the Sun as a self-luminous body. The planets, however, do not shine by their own light and are therefore not self-luminous. We can only see them because sunlight is reflected off their surfaces. Out in the depths of space there are strange stars (and probably other planets too) of very unusual type

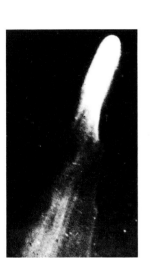

▲Comets, which also belong to the solar system, consist mainly of thin, cold gas, ices and dust. When they come close to the sun, like Halley's Comet as photographed here in 1910, they often produce long spectacular tails.

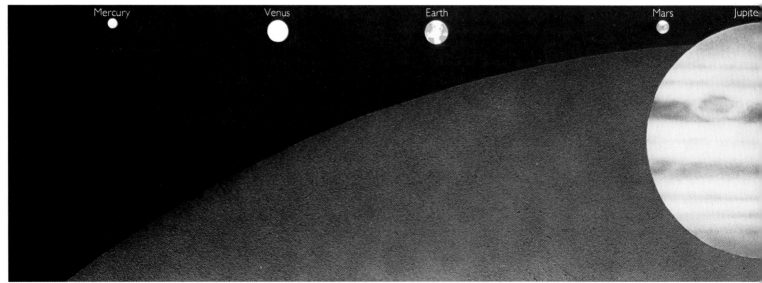

Mercury　　　Venus　　　Earth　　　Mars　　Jupite

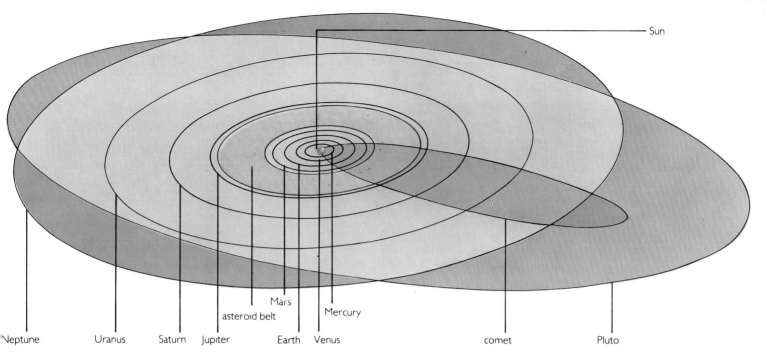

Sun

Mars

asteroid belt

Mercury

Neptune   Uranus   Saturn   Jupiter   Earth   Venus   comet   Pluto

(such as X-ray and infrared stars). Some are quite invisible in the ordinary light our eyes are able to see.

The Zodiac
The ancient sky-watchers noted that the wandering 'stars' moved across the heavens in a narrow band, or belt (*the ecliptic*), which they called the Zodiac. The name Zodiac comes from a Greek work *zodiakos* – meaning 'belonging to the animals'. This is not as strange as it may seem because the Greeks arranged the background stars into groups, or constellations, which to their imaginative minds often took on the fanciful figures of

animals and human figures, and they made up many stories and legends about them. The Zodiac consists of 12 constellations and each, as well as a figure or animal form, also has its own symbol – referred to as its sign in the Zodiac.

If you read that the Sun, a planet or the Moon is entering a particular sign, it means it is passing in front of that background constellation. However, when the Sun enters and crosses a sign, we cannot see the background stars because, although the stars still shine in the daylight sky, they are blotted out by the overpowering light of the Sun. Only at the time of a total eclipse of the Sun, when the Moon passes briefly in front of it, can we see bright stars in daytime. Stories that stars can be seen in broad daylight by looking up from the bottom of a deep pit or mine shaft are untrue.

▲The eight major planets, Mercury, Venus, Earth, Mars, Jupiter, Saturn, Uranus and Neptune, all travel round the Sun in slightly egg-shaped (elliptical) orbits which lie approximately in the same flat plane. However, the orbits of both Chiron and Pluto and many asteroids and comets are by comparison very erratic (eccentric). Comets, in particular, have very elongated orbits which stretch out to or beyond the fringes of the solar system into deep space.

▼The relative sizes of the major planets in comparison with the Sun. We now know that Jupiter and Uranus have rings

round them. Neptune may have rings too, but they are very faint and cannot be seen with ordinary telescopes.

Saturn   Uranus   Neptune   Pluto

OUR SUN AS A STAR

corona

chromosphere   photosphere   prominence   sunspot

energy-producing core

▲A section taken through the Sun to show its different zones, or shells, and the flame-like prominences.

Sol, our star, is just one among the millions of stars in our own galaxy, the Milky Way, and one among the billions of stars in the universe.

As stars rate, our Sun is an average body. Yet to us on Earth, it is by far the most impressive and important object in the sky because its light and heat dominate all our daily activities. Without

the energy from the constant powerhouse of the Sun, life on Earth would not be possible.

The Earth lies from the Sun at an average distance of 148,800,000 km (93,000,000 miles). Even so far away we soak up energy equal to 1,950,000 horsepower per square km (5,000,000 hp per square mile) from its 1,392,000 km

(865,000 mile) diameter surface. But this is only a minute fraction of the Sun's total energy output which radiates into space in all directions. If we could tap all the energy falling over a given area, just a few square kilometres or miles of the Earth's surface could supply as much energy as an atomic power station and would make all power stations obsolete.

We see the Sun shining as a bright orange-red ball and looking about the same size as we see the full Moon. It looks a lot closer than it is. Its remote distance from us can only be truly appreciated when we realise that a jet aircraft, travelling at a constant 1,000 kmph (620 mph), would take almost 17 years to reach its outer surface!

Why the Sun appears red
Light from the Sun is made up of several colours that combine to make white light. However, our atmosphere filters out part of the incoming blue light which makes the Sun, whose real colour is yellow, appear more orange-red than it is. The blue light filtered out is scattered, and this is why the sky is blue in daytime.

At sunrise or sunset the Sun often looks blood-red, and the reason for this is that the sunlight then has to travel through a greater distance of air and dust which causes more filtering and scattering. Because the Earth's atmosphere also bends (refracts) incoming light – and bending is greatest near the horizon – the shape of the Sun at sunrise and sunset will often appear oval, or flattened.

The Sun's heat
How does the Sun generate its great heat? And why does it not quickly burn out as, for example, it would if made of a substance like coal? This remained a mystery until scientists understood atomic energy. Before this some scientists believed the Sun could not be older than 20 million years. They were wrong. We now know the Sun is much older and is a kind of atomic power station which has been producing huge amounts of energy for thousands of millions of years. It has been calculated that every second it radiates into space as much energy as

that of the simultaneous explosion of several billion atomic bombs.

On its surface the Sun's normal temperature is about 6,000°C, but the temperature increases rapidly towards its centre to reach 15,000,000°C. The Sun differs from solid planets like the Earth because it is made mostly of hydrogen gas. Inside there are different zones, or shells.

The corona is the Sun's outermost atmospheric zone. Even this is a very hot region and in parts of it the temperature may reach 1,000,000°C.

The solar wind
The most impressive activities we can see on the Sun are dark red swirling clouds of hot hydrogen gas which look exactly like gigantic flames. These are called prominences and may burst out from the surface to a height of several hundred thousand km/miles, travelling at speeds over 160 km (100 miles) per second.

When prominences occur, showers of broken hydrogen atoms are shot out into space and form what is called the solar wind. Many of these tiny particles travel out far beyond the orbit of Mars. On the way some are attracted by the Earth's magnetic poles and cause displays of colourful Northern and Southern lights (the aurorae) in our atmosphere. When the solar wind is active, it may be a radiation danger to astronauts in orbit round the Earth. The solar wind is also responsible for producing spectacular comet tails when these bodies are near the Sun.

Sunspots
Some of the most interesting of the visible features on the Sun's surface are dark spots that appear from time to time. These are the so-called sunspots.

Although they first attracted general attention in about 1610, shortly after the telescope was invented, there are many records that they were seen with the naked eye in ancient China, Japan and Korea. In addition, the Greek scholar Theophrastus noted them in about 300 BC. It is also most likely that the astronomer-priests of ancient Britain saw them when the Sun rose over the Heel

The sunlight we see now is the result of nuclear reactions which took place deep in the core of the Sun millions of years ago. Indeed, sunlight is 'fossil' evidence of the Sun's past atomic history.

▼Sunspots were first seen by the ancient sky-watchers. Although the spots appear dark at the centre, they are still very hot.

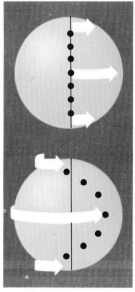

▲The Sun rotates faster at its equator than in its polar regions. Because of this, sunspots after several rotations will appear to drift in a curved pattern.

CAUTION!
In spite of the Sun's great distance, NEVER look at it directly with the naked eye, through binoculars or a telescope as this may lead to permanent blindness.

Even specially manufactured sun-filters are not entirely safe, and smoked glass is *not* recommended. If you want to observe sunspots, the best method is to project the Sun's image through a small telescope onto a white card as in the photograph opposite top. This safe way of observing sunspots was invented by the famous Italian astronomer Galileo back in 1610.

Stone at Stonehenge on midsummer mornings as long ago as 2500–1500 BC.

But what are those spots? Even today we are not completely certain. What is known, however, is that they are whirlpool-like features in the Sun's outer shell, probably caused by activities inside the Sun.

In 1843 a German amateur astronomer, Heinrich Schwabe (1789–1875), announced that he had observed the Sun with his small telescope on every possible day for 43 years and recorded the number of spots visible. As a result he noted the spots appeared to be more frequent and then less frequent in a cycle of 11 years. His discovery was confirmed by other astronomers and this is now called the solar cycle.

A typical sunspot consists of two main parts: a completely dark centre (called the *umbra* – Latin for 'shade') surrounded by a less dark zone (called the *penumbra* – Latin for 'almost shade'). Although the middle part of a sunspot appears black, it is still a very hot region of about 4,000°C. Sunspots only appear dark due to contrast because they are slightly cooler than the surrounding surface which is about 6,000°C.

Some sunspots are born and die away within a matter of hours while others grow and persist for weeks or months. Some reach millions of square kilometres/ miles in size and are large enough to engulf the Earth many times over.

Because the Sun, like the Earth, spins on its axis, sunspots can been seen to shift from day to day in an east to west direction. However, the Sun's surface is not rigid. At its equator sunspots rotate in about 25 days, but towards the polar regions this period gradually lengthens to 33 days.

Birth and death of the Sun
Astronomers believe the Sun has been shining like it does today for several thousand million years – since it was born out of an interstellar gas cloud. Nevertheless, it cannot go on burning for ever. Every second it uses up 600 million tons of its hydrogen supply and therefore has a measurable life span. Like all other stars the Sun slowly evolves from one state to another. In the far future, perhaps in 5,000 million years, it will have burnt up all its hydrogen and will begin to expand like a balloon. First it will engulf Mercury, then Venus and finally our own planet. By then it will have grown into a star known as a red giant. Long before then life on Earth will have become extinct, and the solar system will be a very different place.

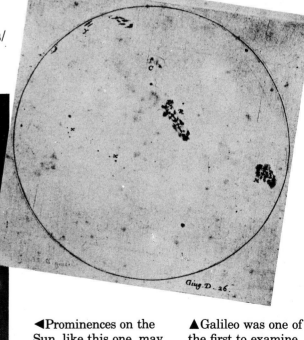

◄Prominences on the Sun, like this one, may cause magnetic disturbances in the Earth's atmosphere and interfere with radio reception.

▲Galileo was one of the first to examine sunspots using a telescope and he made several drawings of them. This one dates from 1613.

▲Safe method of projecting the Sun's image to view sunspots.

◀ Birth and death of a star larger than the Sun:

1 Part of a large hydrogen gas and dust cloud begins to contract under its own gravitational attraction. As it does so, the centre grows hotter...

2 When the core of the new star is sufficiently hot and dense, its nuclear furnaces begin to burn and hydrogen turns into helium. The star begins to shine...

3 After about 150 million years or so the star swells to become a supergiant. It starts to turn helium into heavier and heavier elements. Metals like iron are manufactured in its 'factory'...

4 The star explodes into a supernova. It scatters the elements it has manufactured in its interior, and these intermingle with interstellar gas and dust.

5 A dark, dense pulsar (neutron star) remains. It may keep on shrinking and, because it is so dense even light from its surface cannot escape, it will finally become a black hole in space...

6 As with the beginning of the supergiant star, a cloud of gas and dust condenses. Because this time the cloud is smaller, a smaller star is born and its life will be longer...

7 The star's furnaces ignite after 100 million years. It will then shine steadily for thousands of millions of years...

8 After a life of perhaps 15,000 million years it will grow old and start to run out of hydrogen. Then it will begin to swell and slowly turn into a red giant – swallowing up its closest planets if it has any orbiting it...

9 It will remain a red giant for a comparatively short time. The central parts will begin to contract, and this will trigger the manufacture of oxygen, neon, magnesium, silicon and iron in its internal 'factory'...

10 Inevitably it will collapse inwards and turn into a white dwarf. Slowly it will cool – turning from white to yellow, then red. At its final stage it will no longer shine and it ends its life as an invisible black dwarf.

PLANETARY ORBITS AND GRAVITY

Even Copernicus did not get his ideas about the Sun and its family of revolving planets quite right. From early Greek times it was assumed that when one body revolved about another, its path, or orbit, would always be in a perfect circle. Copernicus, too, believed this was true. It was Johannes Kepler (1571–1631), Tycho's pupil, who found that this was incorrect.

Tycho Brahe had carefully measured the shift of Mars against the background stars. When he died, still believing in the Ptolemaic system, Kepler inherited these observations and used them for some calculations. He became puzzled, for, according to his figures, Mars did not move in a perfect circle round the Sun. Instead its path was very nearly the shape of a *flattened* circle – an ellipse. He recalculated, but there was no mistake. Kepler now realised that instead of revolving in circles, Mars and the other planets revolved in orbits shaped like ellipses.

As a result of this discovery, Kepler worked out three very important laws (now called Kepler's Laws) and drew up tables for planetary movements. The modern calculations necessary to put astronauts into space owe a very great deal to the three basic laws carefully worked out by Kepler over 350 years ago.

Universal gravitation

Although Copernicus and Kepler discovered much about how the planets moved round the Sun, they did not understand what kept them in orbit and why they did not fall into the Sun. The Italian astronomer Galileo Galilei (1564–1642) experimented with gravity by dropping different weights from the Leaning Tower of Pisa, but he did not try to discover if the force of gravity also acted on bodies outside the Earth. This was left to the Englishman Isaac Newton (1642–1727) who was born the year Galileo died.

The story that watching an apple fall from a tree in his orchard set Newton thinking about the force of gravity is true. Part of the actual tree is still preserved at the Royal Astronomical Society in London. However, it took Newton another 20 years to work out the detailed theory of universal gravitation – the force that affects everything in motion in the universe.

Newton knew it was the force of gravity that pulled the apple down. But, if the Earth had pulled the apple down, could the Earth also pull on the Moon in the sky? This in turn made him wonder why the Moon kept going round the Earth and why the Earth and other planets kept going round the Sun. After all, they were not roped, or chained. Why did they not move in straight paths and wander off into space?

Newton pondered a long time and invented some new mathematics to solve the problem. He was greatly helped in his work by Kepler's Three Laws and by the encouragement of his friend Edmond Halley (1656–1742), an English astronomer who later made good use of Newton's discoveries in his work on comets. With Halley's help and encouragement, Newton published the results of his work in 1687 in a book written in Latin (like all important scientific books then) and called *Principia*.

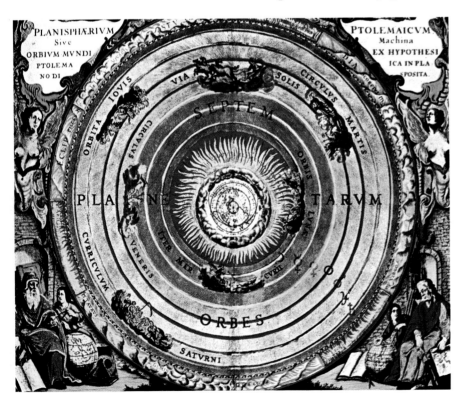

▼This 17th-century print illustrates Ptolemy's theory that the Earth was the centre of the Universe and that everything else revolved around it.

A revolutionary idea

Newton's discoveries were the greatest step forward astronomy has ever known. He stated the most important part of his work in three laws – now referred to as Newton's Laws. In working out these laws, Newton had discovered the startling fact that when the apple in his orchard was pulled down by the Earth, *the apple was also pulling the Earth upwards.* He found the apple was pulling the Earth with just the same force the Earth was pulling the apple. Stated another way it means: when an apple falls from a tree to the ground, the Earth starts to 'fall' upwards to meet it. However, the massive Earth is shifted by an amount too small to be measured. From his observations of the apple he derived his Third Law which states: Every action has an equal and opposite reaction.

But just as the apple pulled at the Earth, Newton found the Moon also pulled at the Earth and likewise the Earth pulled back with an equal force. However, the pull of the Moon has a much greater effect on the Earth than the pull of an apple. It makes the oceans bulge as the Earth spins on its axis and so causes tides. Thus Newton also discovered why the oceans have tides.

Newton found that all the Sun's attendants are kept in orbit by the force of gravity and that the strength of gravity depends on the size, or mass, of the object being attracted. For example, as Jupiter is a giant planet, much larger than the Earth, its gravity-pull is much stronger than the Earth's.

Yet another aspect of gravity is its effect on weight. The Moon is much smaller than the Earth, and therefore its mass is less. As a result an astronaut standing on the Moon weighs only one-sixth of what he weighs on Earth and so can jump much higher. On some of the tiny asteroids the force of gravity is so weak that a future astronaut landing on one would be able to leap off again into space.

Gravity is everywhere in the universe. Even light from distant stars and galaxies can be bent off course by it. But at great distances it is a weak force. While it is now understood from Newton's work *how* gravity works, we still do not properly understand exactly *what* it is. Albert Einstein (1879–1955), one of the greatest modern scientists, discovered some modifications to Newton's ideas, but they did not alter Newton's Laws for everyday purposes.

▲In this picture from an old book we see standing (from left to right) Galileo, Kepler, Tycho Brahe, Copernicus and Ptolemy.

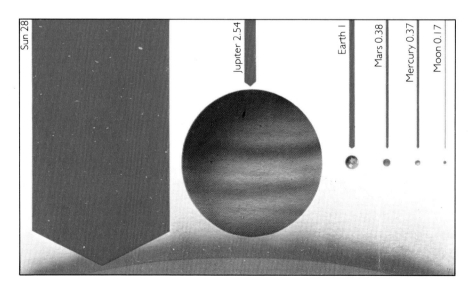

▲The pull of gravity on different members of the solar system depends on their mass.

17

THE INNER PLANETS

▼Compared with the Earth, Mercury is a small planet, and its diameter is not much greater than the width of the Atlantic Ocean.

▶The Mariner space probes revealed that Mercury's surface is similar to the Moon's.

Mercury

Mercury is the closest known planet to the Sun and takes 88 days to revolve round it. It is a small planet with a diameter of 4,880 km (3,025 miles). Because it is always near to the Sun, it can be difficult to spot with the naked eye. The best time to look for it is before dawn or just after sunset when it is suitably positioned in its orbit. Compared with the Earth it spins very slowly on its axis, taking 59 Earth days to do so.

Little was known about its surface until the unmanned American Mariner probes reached it in 1974 and 1975. The pictures sent back to Earth showed its surface to be peppered with craters just like our own Moon. Also like our own Moon, Mercury is a dead world without

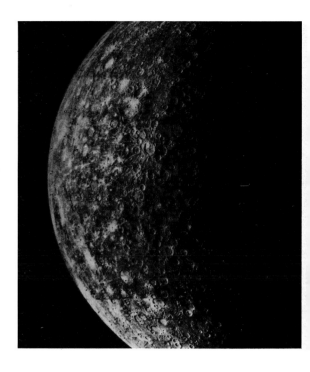

atmosphere.

Astronomers now believe that all the inner planets, including Earth, were heavily bombarded and cratered by asteroid-like objects early in their histories. Except in a few cases, erosion – working over eons of time – has eradicated most traces of this on Earth.

Being so close to the Sun, Mercury's surface in its daytime is baked in a furnace heat hot enough to melt lead and set fire to wood. By contrast the temperature in the nighttime drops to as low as −175°C, much colder than anything on Earth.

Photographs of Mercury's pock-marked surface show it to have enormously steep cliffs over 500 km (300 miles) long and 4 km (2½ miles) high. These run across mountains and craters alike and were probably caused when the surface began to shrink.

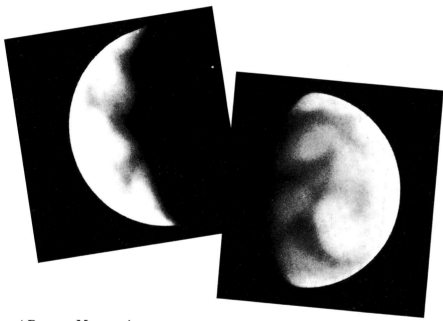

▲Because Mercury is inside the Earth's orbit, closer to the Sun, it has phases like the Moon.

◀Mercury's orbit is more oval (eccentric) than the Earth's and more steeply inclined to the normal paths of the planets (the ecliptic).

deadly sulphuric acid clouds which rain down in torrents on the arid sun-baked surface while fierce lightning storms rage.

Venus's surface, like Mercury's, is ocean-less and also cratered. Some craters are formed by huge volcanoes and others are the result of impacts by asteroids. Mountains tower 10–15 km (6–9½ miles) high – much higher than Everest. No living thing survives on Venus. Its atmosphere is so dense that the pressure there is 1,260 pounds per square inch compared with a mere 14 pounds on Earth. Thus, if an astronaut ever landed on Venus, he would be subject to 90 times more pressure than he was used to back home on Earth and would be crushed to death unless properly protected.

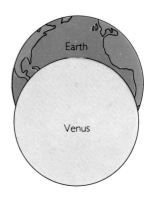

◀This photograph of Venus's cloud-covered surface was taken from a distance of 720,000 km (450,000 miles) by the space probe Mariner 10 when it was on its way to Mercury in 1974.

▲Venus is a planet only slightly smaller than the Earth. Because its surface is permanently covered by thick clouds, nothing can ever be seen of its surface through earth-bound telescopes.

Venus

As viewed from Earth, Venus is by far the brightest planet, and we can often see it before the Sun has set (but remember not to look directly at the Sun).

After Mercury, it is the next planet out from the Sun and is 108.2 million km (67.26 million miles) from it. It is just slightly smaller than the Earth with a diameter of 12,100 km (7,500 miles). Its journey round the Sun takes 224.7 days. Unlike the Earth, it spins very slowly on its axis – just once every 243 Earth days. As a result, the side of the planet facing the Sun becomes overheated. This creates fantastically high winds which blow through Venus's dense atmosphere at speeds up to 350 km (220 miles) per hour – or three times the speed of the worst hurricane-force winds we have on Earth.

Because Venus is permanently shrouded in dense clouds, astronomers in the past often called it the Veiled Planet or the Planet of Mystery. Modern space probes changed that when they finally penetrated its deadly atmosphere. None of the early space probes survived long enough to give much information about the searing heat of its surface. However, later ones confirmed the planet is extremely hot – up to 460°C. These probes also revealed that the thick atmosphere consists of carbon dioxide and

▲Like Mercury, Venus lies inside the Earth's orbit, closer to the Sun, and therefore shows phase effects as does the Moon. As it appears here it is almost in line with the Earth and the Sun. When Galileo discovered this phase effect, he saw at once proof that Copernicus was right: Venus revolves round the Sun and not the Earth as Ptolemy had thought.

EARTH-MOON SYSTEM

Astronomers usually treat the Moon as a satellite of the Earth because it revolves round us (in 29½ days), but the two can also be thought of as twin planets. Nevertheless, as twins there are great differences – just as there are great differences between Earth and the rest of the planets. Since recent space probes have shown that the chances of finding life elsewhere in the solar system are remote, our Earth has been nicknamed the Planet of Life.

After the Sun, the Moon is the most influential body acting on the Earth. It lies 384,000 km (238,000 miles) distant which may seem a long way but it is actually very close when compared with Venus and Mars, the next nearest objects to Earth. The Moon revolves counter-clockwise round the Earth in a period of 29 days 12 hr 44 min, and during this time its illuminated face changes shape as we see different parts of it.

Phases of the Moon

When New Moon occurs, the Moon lies in the direction of the Sun, and we cannot see it because its illuminated face is towards the Sun. A few days later, as it moves on in its orbit round the Earth, we

►The Earth is often called the 'Planet of Life'. Seen here between the cloud gaps is the whole of the Mediterranean, North Africa, the Red Sea and Arabia. By comparison the Moon is a much smaller world and completely arid and lifeless.

begin to see it as a very thin crescent in the western sky after sunset. Although people usually refer to this thin crescent as the New Moon, it is actually by now several days old.

At this time we may see the dark, unlit part faintly illuminated by sunlight reflected off the Earth. In the old days people used to say this was the Old Moon cradled in the arms of the New Moon.

As the Moon continues on its monthly journey, the crescent shape waxes, or grows bigger, as we see more of the Moon's sunlit face. When we see half the Moon's sunlit face, this is called First Quarter. It may seem strange to call half the Moon 'a quarter', but in terms of the whole Moon the illuminated part *visible to us* is only a quarter. About seven days later we see the whole of the Moon's sunlit face and this is called Full Moon.

After Full Moon, as the Moon travels on, its sunlit face begins to wane, or shrink. When it shrinks to exactly half, this is called Last Quarter. From Last Quarter, as it creeps closer to the Sun, it will become crescent-shaped again until it finally disappears from view in the dawn sky near the time of the next New Moon.

Because the Moon keeps its same face

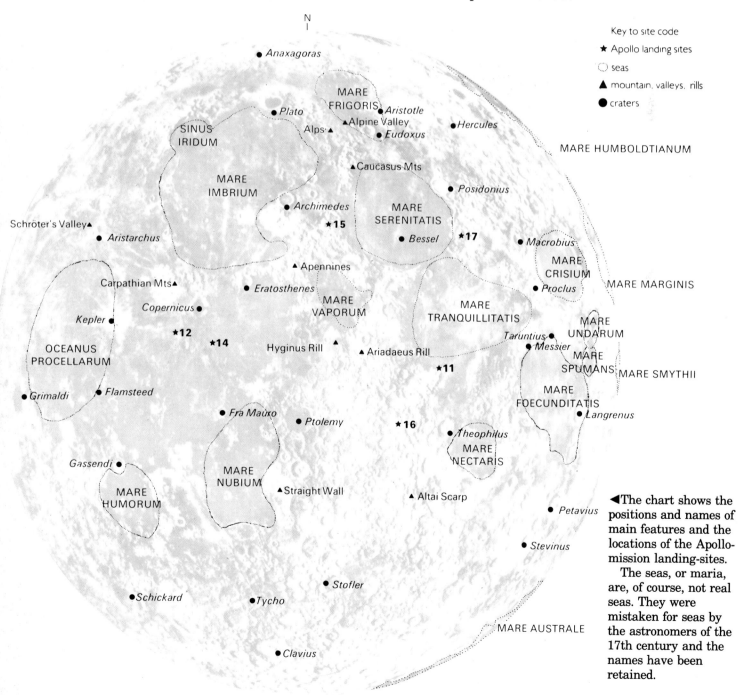

Key to site code
★ Apollo landing sites
◌ seas
▲ mountain, valleys, rills
● craters

◀The chart shows the positions and names of main features and the locations of the Apollo-mission landing-sites.

The seas, or maria, are, of course, not real seas. They were mistaken for seas by the astronomers of the 17th century and the names have been retained.

pointing towards the Earth as it *revolves* round us (in 29½ days), it also has *rotated* once in that time. The Moon does this because it is 'locked' in the Earth's more powerful gravitational pull. Until space probes were sent behind the Moon, we had no way of knowing what the surface on the other side of it looked like.

The Moon and the Earth

Compared with the Earth the Moon is a small body. Its diameter is 3,476 km (2,159 miles) which is less than Mercury's. Even so the Moon's gravitational pull is strong enough to cause tides. Although the ancient Greeks realised that the Moon had *something* to do with tides, they could not explain why it had. This was done by Isaac Newton during his research into universal gravitation (p 16). Tides also affect the Moon, but since it has no surface water the Earth's pull lifts its solid crust – sometimes by several metres – so that Moon-quakes result.

The Moon is a dead and arid world. No life of any kind has ever existed there. It has no atmosphere, and its surface is heavily cratered. It has remained a largely unchanged world for almost 4,000 million years (4 eons) since soon after it came into being. This occurred perhaps 4.5 eons ago at the same time as its big sister planet, Earth. But how the Moon and the Earth were born remains one of the mysteries of astronomy.

The Moon's features

Before space probes reached the Moon, all our knowledge of it was gained by looking at it through telescopes. When astronomers like Galileo began to observe it with the newly invented telescope in about 1610, some imagined the dark areas were seas. They were therefore called *maria* (Latin for 'seas'). Although astronomers now know there is no water on the Moon's surface, the traditional names have been retained on maps. When the Moon is full, these 'seas' suggest fanciful figures and shapes such as 'the Man in the Moon', 'the Woman bent reading a book' or 'the Crab's Claw'.

In addition to the dark maria regions, which are really old lava plains, there is

◀Because the Moon keeps the same face towards the Earth, we never see its far side. This picture is from the Apollo 16 mission in April 1972.

a great variety of craters and crater-like features. Some seem to be more recent than others, and new ones have often partially destroyed older ones. How all these different features were formed is still not certain. Some are due to impact by giant meteorites and asteroids; others are volcanic features but different from those on Earth. Along the borders of the maria, mountains rise steeply to over 7,000 metres (23,000 feet).

The arrival of the Apollo 11 mission astronauts on 20 July 1969 heralded the most important period of the Moon's history. Rock samples were collected and brought back to Earth and examined by experts in many countries. Although these moon-rocks provided much new information, they also raised many fresh queries about the origins of the Moon and the Earth.

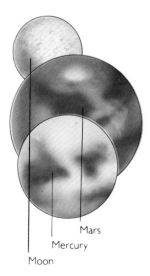

▲The size of the Moon compared with that of Mercury and Mars. In some ways the Moon resembles these other cratered planets.

23

ECLIPSES

There are two kinds of eclipses; solar and lunar. By a remarkable astronomical coincidence the *apparent* size of the Moon is approximately equal to that of the Sun. The Moon is, of course, much smaller than the Sun and only appears as large since it is much nearer to us.

Because the Moon's orbit round the Earth is oval-shaped, or elliptical, the Moon is not always the same distance from Earth. Therefore the Moon sometimes seems to us smaller than the Sun and at other times larger. This produces different kinds of eclipse of the Sun.

Solar eclipses

Eclipses of the Sun occur when the Moon comes *exactly* in line between the Earth and the Sun. It does not do this every New Moon because as well as being elliptical-shaped, the Moon's orbit is slightly tilted. Only when the Moon passes at a crossing-point (called a node) in its orbit at the time of New Moon can a total eclipse of the Sun occur. Then, if the Moon is apparently larger than the Sun, the Sun will be covered, or *totally* eclipsed, when the Moon passes in front of it. When the Moon appears slightly smaller, a narrow width of Sun will be left showing round the edge of the Moon. This is called an *annular* (Latin, meaning 'ring-like') eclipse. If the Sun and Moon are not exactly in line, only part of the Sun is covered and a partial eclipse is seen.

Total eclipses of the Sun are much more impressive events than annular or partial eclipses. At time of totality the whole sky darkens, and bright stars and planets become visible. Birds, thinking the Sun has set and night is falling, fly to their nests.

Lunar eclipses

Lunar eclipses occur when the Earth comes in line between the Moon and the Sun at the time of Full Moon and casts its shadow across the Moon. As the Earth's shadow creeps slowly across the Moon's surface, it has a distinct curved edge. This was proof to the early Greeks that the Earth was a round body. Like solar eclipses, lunar eclipses are sometimes only partial ones when the Sun, Earth and Moon are not exactly in line.

▼The impressive 'diamond-ring' effect shown here occurs just before the Moon obscures the Sun at the time of a total eclipse of the Sun. It occurs again just after the Moon begins to move away.

MARS

Moving out from the Earth-Moon system, the next planet from the Sun is Mars – often referred to as the Red Planet because of its very distinct red colour.

Before the modern space age it was widely believed that some kind of life existed there. Some astronomers even claimed to have observed canal-like features criss-crossing the surface. These they supposed were great waterways constructed by the planet's intelligent inhabitants to bring water from the Martian polar caps to the darker regions thought to be areas of vegetation.

Speculation ended when the American Mariner probes reached Mars in 1964, 1965 and 1971 and then the Viking probes in 1975. Instead of a planet with intelligent life they found an arid, cratered wasteland with very little atmosphere and no running surface water. The so-called canals had been figments of the imagination. The special automatic sampler devices, landed on the surface to check for signs of living matter, have not yet detected any trace of life. What water Mars has is frozen into its thin polar caps or locked away below its chill surface as permafrost.

Mars is smaller than the Earth with a diameter of 6,800 km (4,200 miles). It spins on its axis in 24 hr 37 min 23 sec, and its axis is tilted 23°59′ – both features remarkably similar to the Earth's. At the average distance from the Sun of 228 million km (142 million miles), its journey round it takes 1.88 Earth years.

While astronomers were disappointed not to find any sign of life on Mars, it seems probable that rivers once flowed there but have now dried up. Fiery, now extinct, volcanoes of great size burnt over a wide area of the planet, and even today gigantic dust storms rage for months on end obscuring the surface.

Mars has two tiny moons called Phobos and Deimos, but from Earth these can only be seen through large telescopes. Both, like Mars itself, are arid worlds, and in close-up photographs taken during space missions, they appear as cratered potato-shaped objects.

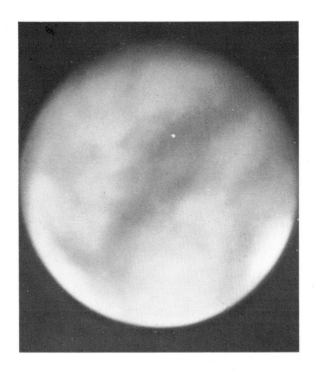

▲A photographic view of Mars taken from Earth shows it to be an orange-red planet with darker areas. The polar cap shown here is its southern one.

▼Phobos, photographed here by Mariner 9, is the larger of the two Martian moons with a diameter of 23 km (14 miles). It revolves round Mars in 7 hr 39 min.

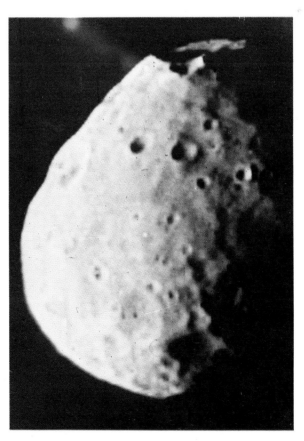

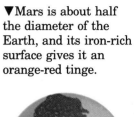

▼Mars is about half the diameter of the Earth, and its iron-rich surface gives it an orange-red tinge.

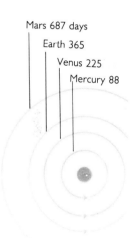

Mars 687 days

Earth 365

Venus 225

Mercury 88

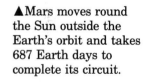

▲Mars moves round the Sun outside the Earth's orbit and takes 687 Earth days to complete its circuit.

25

THE GIANT PLANETS

Ganymede
Callisto
Io
Europa

Jupiter

Jupiter, or Zeus as the Greeks called him, was chief of the ancient gods, and it is appropriate his name should be given to the largest planet.

Jupiter's massive bulk is about $2\frac{1}{2}$ times greater than all the other planets put together. It is an oval-shaped body measuring 142,800 km (88,700 miles) across its equatorial regions and 134,200 km (81,960 miles) across its polar regions. Even through a very small telescope, or powerful binoculars, its polar regions look distinctly flattened.

Jupiter rotates faster than any other planet, taking 9 hr 50 min at its equator and 9 hr 55 min near its poles. This difference in times indicates that Jupiter's visible surface, unlike the inner planets', is not fixed. The colourful belts we see around Jupiter are the outer regions of an enormously thick atmosphere. One of the most striking features of the belts is the famous Red Spot — although it does not always look red. It has a large oval shape, but unlike the ever-changing cloud belts, it maintains its form over a long time. Space probes have confirmed that the Red Spot is a huge hurricane-like disturbance in Jupiter's atmosphere.

Jupiter's moons

Jupiter takes 11.86 Earth years to revolve round the Sun at a distance of 750 million km (460 million miles). On its journey it is accompanied by a family of at least 16 moons and probably by some tiny ones yet undiscovered. Four of its moons are large bodies. The one called Ganymede is 5,280 km (3,275 miles) in diameter which is larger than either Mercury or our Moon.

Galileo discovered the four largest moons in 1610. Through ordinary binoculars they appear as tiny, bright specks hugging their parent planet. Night to night observation will reveal them constantly shifting position as they orbit Jupiter.

The American Pioneer and Voyager space missions have given us much more information about Jupiter and its large family of moons. At its centre, Jupiter probably has a rocky core somewhat larger than the Earth. Above this is a great thickness of liquid hydrogen under high pressure. Electric storms rage constantly in its atmosphere, and no matter what science-fiction writers invent about it, Jupiter is a very cold and inhospitable place and quite different from the cosy world of the Earth.

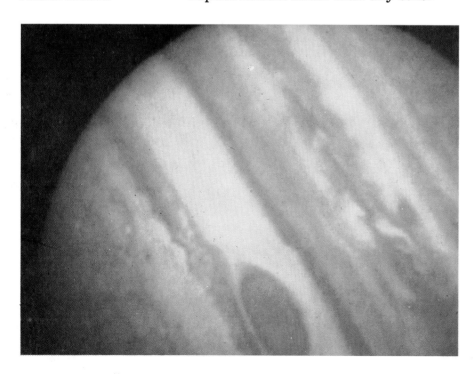

Saturn

◀A comparison of the sizes of Saturn and the Earth (the blue sphere).

▶Saturn's rings are tilted and stay at the same angle so that, when sometimes viewed from Earth, they may be seen edge on as in 'a' when the planet is in that part of its orbit. In 'b' the rings will be tilted towards us and will appear open as in the photograph **below**.

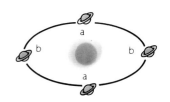

Astronomers consider Saturn to be the show-piece of the sky, and for good reasons they have nicknamed it 'Lord of the Rings'. Even through a small telescope its spectacular ring system provides a constant source of wonder.

Saturn is the largest planet after Jupiter. Its equatorial diameter is 119,400 km (74,150 miles), but because it is even more flattened than Jupiter, its diameter pole to pole is only 106,900 km (66,400 miles). Its oval shape is a result of its fast rotation which occurs in 10 hr 14 min. Its journey round the Sun takes 29.59 years.

In many ways Saturn is similar to Jupiter. Both are chilly, hostile worlds. Like Jupiter, Saturn has a very thick atmosphere. At its centre lies a rocky core, a little larger than the Earth, which is surrounded by a deep layer of hydrogen in its metallic form. Immediately below its atmosphere may be a vast ocean of liquid hydrogen plus other compounds.

Although Saturn is a large, bulky planet, it is very light in weight. If it were possible to find an ocean large enough, Saturn would float on it while the much denser, smaller Earth would sink like a stone.

In 1980 pictures from the American Voyager mission revealed the detailed wonders of the rings in close-up for the first time. It was discovered they have a very complicated structure and are only a few hundred metres/yards thick. For the most part they probably consist of myriads of small hailstones, all jostling in orbit round Saturn like tiny separate moons packed close together.

Saturn also has a family of larger moons. The biggest, Titan, is almost a planet in its own right. It measures 5,500 km (3,400 miles) in diameter and has a dense atmosphere. As it seems to be permanently shrouded in thick clouds, no view of its surface has been obtained yet. Titan is bright enough to be glimpsed very near Saturn through a small telescope about the size of that used to project the Sun's image (p 15).

▼The photograph clearly shows Saturn to be flattened at its poles due to its fast rotation – making the equatorial regions bulge out. Cloud belts on Saturn are less colourful and distinct than those on Jupiter. Saturn's ring system is a complicated structure and several distinct zones, or divisions, occur. Note Saturn's own shadow cast onto its rings to the left of the planet.

▶About every 15 years or so, Saturn's rings are tilted towards the Earth and astronomers can get a good view of them. When they are edge on to us, they are invisible. These apparent changes to Saturn puzzled early astonomers like Galileo.

◀ Uranus has five moons circling it in periods ranging from 1½ to just over 13 days. The planet itself takes 84 years to go round the Sun once.

▼ Uranus is a peculiar planet because, unlike the Earth which spins on its axis almost upright at 23½°, Uranus's poles are tilted over to 98°.

Uranus

Uranus and Neptune are two planets of a kind. Both were discovered telescopically and are about equal in size. Uranus is

slightly larger than Neptune; its diameter is 52,000 km (32,240 miles); it rotates in 15½ hours; and revolves round the Sun in 84 earth-years.

Although Uranus was discovered in 1781 by William Herschel (1738–1822), a musician and amateur astronomer, it is sometimes possible to glimpse it with the naked eye if you know its exact position. In some ways Uranus is a peculiar planet. Its polar regions are tilted over (98°) to where one would normally expect to find the equatorial regions. Another surprising feature is its ring system, discovered in 1977. Until then it was thought that Saturn was the only planet surrounded by rings. However, observing Uranus using special methods, astronomers detected several narrow rings separated by wide gaps. Further knowledge of these mysterious rings, and the exploration of its family of five moons, awaits the Voyager 2 space mission due to pass close to Uranus in 1986.

▼Neptune is a much larger body than the Earth. It is not visible to the naked eye but it can be seen as a faint 'star' with quite a small telescope if you know its exact position.

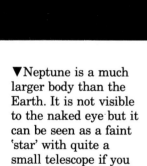

Neptune

While the telescopic discovery of Uranus was accidental, that of Neptune was not. Two men, Urbain Le Verrier (1811–77), a Frenchman, and John Couch Adams (1819–92), an Englishman, independently calculated that another planet must exist beyond Uranus. After a short search it was found in 1846 by the German

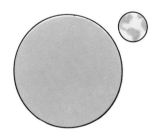

▶Neptune and its two moons Triton and Nereid. Triton, slightly larger than our Moon, is hugging the planet. Nereid (arrowed) is only 240 km (150 miles) in diameter.

astronomer Johann Galle (1812–1910) and his assistant, Heinrich D'Arrest (1822–75) almost in the position Le Verrier and Adams had predicted.

Neptune is the most distant of the giant planets. Its diameter is 48,400 km (30,000 miles), and it takes 165 Earth years to go round the Sun. It rotates once in 18¼ hours.

Little is known about its cloud-covered surface and its two moons. Further knowledge, in particular whether it also has a faint ring system like Uranus, awaits the Voyager space probes of the future.

It can be an exciting experience to make a telescopic discovery of Neptune for yourself – just as Galle and D'Arrest did in 1846. What is required is a detailed sky map showing faint stars and some up-to-date information about Neptune's exact position. Only a small telescope is required – the kind shown for projecting the Sun (p 15) is big enough.

Pluto and Chiron

Pluto and Chiron are the two odd men out among the members of the outer solar system as both are quite small planets. Pluto was discovered in 1930 after a long photographic search by Clyde Tombaugh at the Lowell Observatory in Arizona. Its diameter is uncertain but it is probably about 3,000 km (1,850 miles), and it spins on its axis only once in 153 days. Pluto is the most distant planet known, but because its path round the Sun is very eccentric, it sometimes travels inside the orbit of Neptune. It is doing so at present and will continue to do so for several years.

In 1977 a moon was discovered circling Pluto very closely and this has been given the name Charon – not to be confused with Chiron. Charon is so close to Pluto that some astronomers think it is not a separate body. They believe that Pluto itself may be an irregular-shaped planet like some of the asteroids.

Chiron lies closer to the Sun than Pluto. It was discovered by accident in 1977 at the Mount Palomar Observatory, California, when it was identified as a new planet on a photographic plate. It is much smaller than Pluto but by how much is uncertain. While its orbit normally lies between Saturn and Uranus, its path, like Pluto's, is very eccentric so it can occasionally travel outside the orbit of Uranus or approach within 6 million km (3.7 million miles) of Saturn. It orbits the Sun in 51 years, but little else is known about it. It is probably more like an asteroid than a major planet and may be the largest of a number of tiny bodies lying undiscovered near the fringes of the solar system – or it might even be the extinct core of a previous comet-like object of a type yet unknown to us.

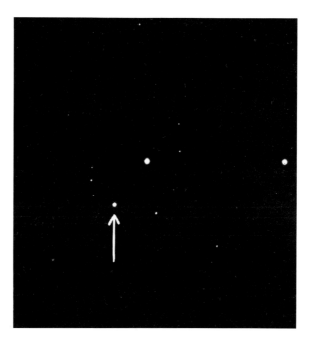

◀Pluto was discovered in 1930 as a result of comparing photographs of the same region of sky on separate nights. During the interval the tiny planet had shifted its position in relation to the background stars and so revealed its presence as a new wanderer.

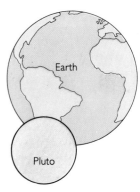

▲The exact diameter of Pluto is still uncertain but it is probably about 3,000 km (1,850 miles). Like Uranus, its polar regions are tipped over on its side.

▶Pluto's steeply inclined orbit round the Sun is at a mean distance of 5,900 million km (3,600 million miles).

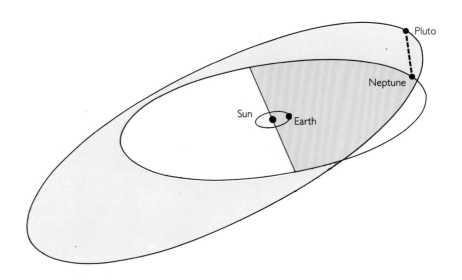

BETWEEN THE PLANETS

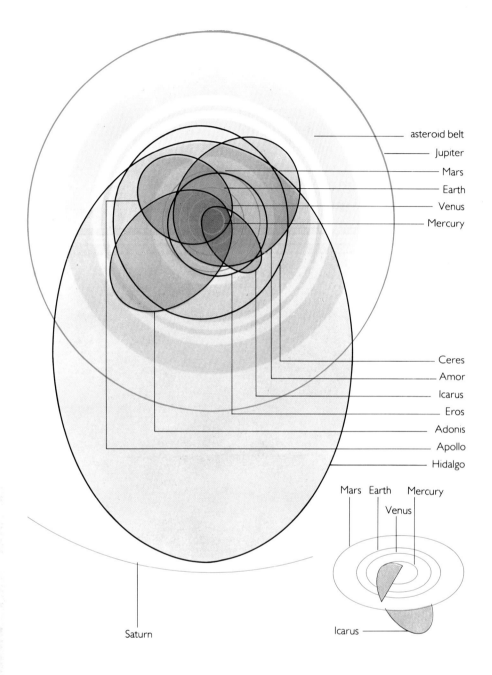

asteroid belt
Jupiter
Mars
Earth
Venus
Mercury

Ceres
Amor
Icarus
Eros
Adonis
Apollo
Hidalgo

Mars   Earth   Mercury
Venus

Icarus

Saturn

Asteroids

The ancient sky-watchers knew only five planets. It was only after Uranus was accidentally discovered by Herschel in 1781 that astronomers started to search for others. Nevertheless, the first of the asteroids, or minor planets as they are sometimes called, was another chance telescopic discovery – made on 1 January 1801 by the Italian astronomer Giuseppe Piazzi (1746–1826). In due course it was named Ceres. Shortly after, more asteroids were found, but Ceres, with a diameter of 995 km (592 miles), proved to be the largest one. At certain times it is possible to glimpse it without a telescope if its exact position is known.

Many thousands of asteroids have now been discovered and named. Most orbit the Sun in a belt called the asteroid belt, or zone, which lies between Mars and Jupiter. However, some of the smaller ones, with diameters of just a kilometre/ mile or so, have very eccentric orbits which take them inside the orbit of Mars. Some even wander inside the orbits of Earth, Venus and Mercury. One such asteroid is Icarus, named after a person in Greek legend who flew too close to the Sun and whose artificial wings melted.

In the past small asteroids have collided with the Earth. The large 'meteorite' crater in Arizona was caused by such an impact. It has been estimated there may be as many as 50,000 asteroids in orbit round the Sun. Most are tiny chunks of rock; some are irregular in shape and at least one of them, Hektor, is a twin object (see Double Stars on p 41). More information about asteroids will come from future space missions.

▲The orbits, or paths, of the asteroids, or minor planets, lie mostly between Mars and Jupiter in a belt, or zone. In the illustration the paths of seven asteroids are shown separately to demonstrate how some of them wander inside the orbit of Mercury and others go out almost to the orbit of Saturn. The inset

shows how the path of Icarus is steeply inclined to the paths of the inner planets.

▶In comparison with the Moon, asteroids are small bodies. Ceres is 955 km (592 miles) in diameter; Pallas 558 km (346 miles); Vesta 555 km (344 miles) and Juno only 249 km (154 miles).

Moon

Ceres Pallas Vesta Juno

Meteors and meteorites

Meteors and meteorites are tiny fragments and chunks of cosmic material which enter the Earth's atmosphere from outer space.

Meteors are usually smaller than a grain of sand. They burn up completely in the atmosphere and leave a brief luminous trail along their flight-path. Meteors were once called falling, or shooting stars. Of course, they are not stars. Mostly they are bits which have broken away from a comet's head (p 32). Millions of meteors enter the Earth's atmosphere every day, but most are too faint to be seen.

Meteors sometimes occur in showers, or storms, and give brilliant displays. One famous shower, the Leonids, takes place at intervals of 33 years and is named after the constellation of Leo, the Lion, from where the meteors appear to emerge. The last spectacular display was in 1966, and another will probably occur in 1999.

Meteorites are pieces of rock and iron which have broken off asteroids. More rarely a small asteroid itself may collide with the Earth and form a huge 'meteorite' crater. The best known of these large craters is in Arizona, and the small asteroid that caused it fell over 25,000 years ago. Another spectacular 'meteorite' fell in Siberia in 1908, but this was a very mysterious object as it left no visible crater.

Small meteorites weighing a few kilogrammes/pounds fall almost every day. Many fall unseen into the oceans or in deserts. Explorers have found hundreds of old meteorites preserved in the ice caps of the polar regions.

In spite of the weight of meteorites and the speed with which they fall, there are no records of a meteorite killing anybody. However, in 1954 in Alabama, USA, a woman was hit on the arm by one. The chance of a personal close encounter with a meteorite is very remote. It has been calculated that in a country the size of the United States a chance will occur *once* in about 9,300 years. There is much more danger in crossing the road!

▼This old print depicts the Leonid meteor shower when it occurred in 1833. One eyewitness reported meteors falling thicker than rain, and people, terrified by the spectacle, are reported to have implored God to save the world and them.

▼The best known meteorite crater lies in the northern Arizona desert. It is 1,260 m (4,134 ft) wide and 170 m (558 ft) deep and was made by an object falling in remote prehistoric times.

◄Halley's Comet passed close to the Sun shortly before the Norman invasion of England in 1066, and is shown in the famous Bayeux Tapestry.

▼Bennett's Comet was a brilliant object in the morning skies of 1970. It was discovered by an amateur astronomer in the southern hemisphere.

▶A photograph of Humason's Comet taken in 1962. It is named after the American who discovered it. In the picture the background stars appear as trails because the camera was made to track on the movement of the comet.

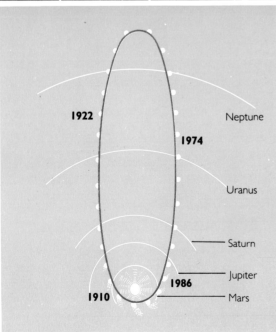

◄The orbit of Halley's famous comet carries it out into the far reaches of the solar system beyond Neptune. It is due to pass close to the Sun in February 1986. On its inward journey it was photographed in late 1982 shining as a very tiny speck.

Comets

Comets are some of the most puzzling objects in the solar system. Even today astronomers are not quite certain what they are or how they were formed.

They appear as very flimsy cloud-like bodies – sometimes with long tails. The head part seems to consist mostly of very thin gas mixed with dust and ice. At the centre of the head most comets probably have a hard, solid lump of matter forming a central nucleus.

Comets may be related to the smaller asteroids. One theory suggests that some of the smallest asteroids are extinct comets – comets which have lost everything except the solid central nucleus – because many comets have orbits similar to asteroids.

The best known comet is Halley's Comet. The English astronomer Edmond Halley did not discover it as many people think. He used Isaac Newton's researches into universal gravitation to calculate the orbit of a comet he and Newton had seen in 1682. He found this was the same comet which appeared in 1607 and was seen by Kepler and before that in 1531 by Petrus Apianus (1495–1552). Halley calculated its future path and found it would appear again in 1758, and so it did. It also appeared in 1066, and an impression of it is in the famous Bayeux Tapestry. Since 1758 it has appeared in 1835 and 1910 and it is due to return to the Sun in 1985–6. In October 1982, still far out in space on its journey back to the Sun, it was photographed as a tiny speck. In 1986 a space probe is due to pass very close to it, and astronomers then hope to learn a lot more about comets.

Near the Sun, bright comets like Halley's develop long tails made of very thin gas and dust, and these appear to stretch right across the sky. Many comets have orbits more eccentric than those of the asteroids and take thousands of years to revolve once round the Sun. A few comets approach the Sun so closely they skim through its atmosphere. These are called Sungrazer comets and are very spectacular objects sometimes visible in broad daylight. The comet with the smallest orbit is Encke's Comet which takes only 3.3 years to go round the Sun.

ORIGIN OF THE SOLAR SYSTEM

One of the most fascinating topics in astronomy is how things began. How the solar system began has puzzled people since the Greeks first thought about the problem over two thousand years ago.

Even today we are not absolutely sure how the Sun and its attendants came to be arranged in their present form. Nevertheless, it seems likely that the Sun condensed out of a great gas and dust cloud very similar to the Great Nebula in Orion we can see today. After the Sun condensed to form a star some of the gas and dust left over began to rotate. Slowly, in the course of time, the gas and dust gathered together (accreted) and formed the solid planetary members of the solar system.

Several theories have been put forward to explain this basic idea. The most widely accepted one was first put forward in the 18th century by the German philospher Immanuel Kant (1724–1804) and the French astronomer Pierre Laplace (1789–1827) and is now called the Kant/Laplace theory.

◄According to the Kant/Laplace theory of the origin of the solar system, it began as a vast cloud of gas. The German philosopher, Kant, thought that the cloud was cool and stationary at first. Later, the French scientist Laplace suggested that it was hot and spinning. It grew steadily hotter until it glowed as the Sun. As the Sun got smaller it spun faster and threw off rings of gas from which the planets formed.

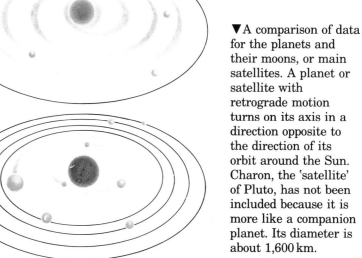

▼A comparison of data for the planets and their moons, or main satellites. A planet or satellite with retrograde motion turns on its axis in a direction opposite to the direction of its orbit around the Sun. Charon, the 'satellite' of Pluto, has not been included because it is more like a companion planet. Its diameter is about 1,600 km.

d = days   h = hours   m = minutes   **r** = retrograde

planet satellites	mean distance from planet (kilometres)	time for one orbit d h m s	mass (Moon=1)	diameter (km)
Earth				
Moon	384,401	27 7 43 12	1·000	3,476
Mars				
I Phobos	9,000	7 39 14	?	14
II Deimos	23,000	1 6 17 55	?	8
Jupiter				
V Amalthea	181,000	10 2 11	?	160
I Io	422,000	1 18 27 34	0·993	3,658
II Europa	671,000	3 13 13 42	0·653	3,100
III Ganymede	1,070,000	7 3 42 33	2·095	5,270
IV Callisto	1,883,000	16 16 32 11	1·293	5,000
VI Hestia	11,476,000	250 13 35	?	100
X Demeter	11,700,000	259 5 15	?	16
VII Hera	11,737,000	259 15 30	?	24
XII Adrastea	21,200,000	630	?	16
XI Pan	22,600,000	692	?	18
VIII Poseidon	23,500,000	739	?	20
IX Hades	23,600,000	758	?	18

planet satellite	mean distance from planet (kilometres)	time for one orbit d h m s	mass (Moon=1)	diameter (km)
Saturn				
X Janus	159,000	17 58 34	?	300
I Mimas	186,000	22 37 5	0·0005	540
II Enceladus	238,000	1 8 53 7	0·001	600
III Tethys	295,000	1 21 18 26	0·009	1,000
IV Dione	377,000	2 17 41 10	0·015	960
V Rhea	527,000	4 10 1 12	0·031	1,300
VI Titan	1,222,000	15 22 41 27	1·864	4,880
VII Hyperion	1,483,000	21 6 38 23	0·001	440
VIII Iapetus	3,560,000	79 7 56 25	0·015	1,100
IX Phoebe	**r** 12,950,000	550 8	?	240
Uranus				
V Miranda	130,000	1 9 56	0·001	240
I Ariel	192,000	2 12 29 21	0·018	700
II Umbriel	267,000	4 3 27 37	0·007	500
III Titania	438,000	8 16 56 28	0·059	1,000
IV Oberon	586,000	13 11 7 6	0·035	900
Neptune				
I Triton	**r** 355,000	5 21 2 13	1·905	3,800
II Nereid	5,562,000	359 23 30	?	240

33

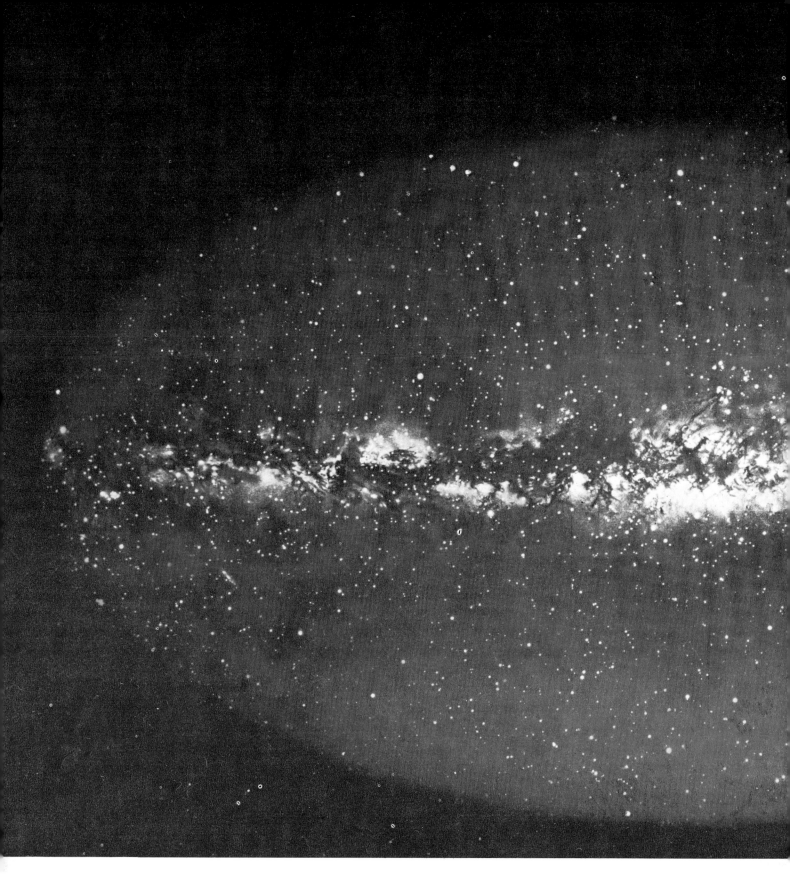

Outdoors on a clear, moonless night, a band of faint milky light is visible right across the heavens. Its position in the sky will depend on the time of night and the season of the year. In winter in the northern hemisphere it will be directly overhead during the early evening, while in summer it will be lower down nearer the northern horizon.

This band of light extends over more than one-tenth of the night sky and represents the galaxy of stars to which the Sun and its attendants belong. Most of the stars in the Milky Way galaxy are concentrated within a narrow band, or plane, and are so distant we cannot see them as separate points of light with the naked eye. The milky appearance is

simply the effect of myriads of faint stars merged together.

To ancient peoples this band of milky light was a great puzzle, and a famous Greek poem refers to it as 'that shining wheel, men call it Milk'. From this the Greeks named it the Galaxy (from *gala* – milk'). However, in the 4th century BC the Greek scholar Democritus guessed its true nature when he wrote: 'It is a lustre of small stars very near together.'

Only when Galileo first turned his new telescope to look at the Milky Way in 1610, was Democritus proved right. Today we know that the Milky Way rotates like a wheel and that the Sun and all its attendants are carried round it once every 200 million years.

▲This remarkable picture represents an overall view of the Milky Way star system – our own galaxy. The Sun and its attendants and all the stars we see in the sky belong to it. Far beyond, in deeper space, are myriads of other milky ways.

THE STARS IN THEIR SEASONS

►The ancient Egyptians also used figures to depict star groups and constellations, but only a few were the same as those used by the Greeks. One Egyptian constellation was the Ox's Foreleg whose stars were used to set the Great Pyramid pointing north in about 2600 BC. This constellation is more familiar to us as the Great Bear or Ursa Major.

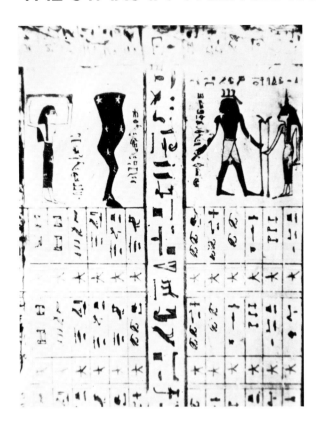

▲A globe showing the heavens made in the 16th century. You can see some of the animal shapes astronomers of the time gave to the constellations.

If you stand outdoors on a starry night, you will in due course notice the stars appear to shift. By watching a particular star, or group of stars, near a tall chimney or building, you will see this motion within a few minutes. A longer spell will show that some stars, like the Sun and Moon, appear to rise in the east, climb up in the sky and then set over the western horizon.

If you look carefully northwards in the northern hemisphere and south in the southern, you will notice some stars which do not rise or set but circle the sky all night long. These are called circumpolar stars because they appear to circle round two pivots in the sky called the north and south celestial poles. What stars you see all night long (circumpolar stars) depends on where you make your observations. For example, looking at the sky from North America or Europe, the constellation of the Great Bear will circle the northern sky continuously and will never be below the horizon – hence it is a circumpolar constellation.

Further observation will reveal that all stars appear to move round the unseen pivots. The height, or altitude, at which these invisible pivots are located depends on your position on the Earth's surface. For example, for someone observing from New York the invisible pivot (the north celestial pole) will be a point about half way between the northern horizon and directly overhead. In the northern hemisphere this invisible pivot is fairly easy to find because fortunately the star Polaris, or the Pole Star, lies very close to it (see star maps).

Of course, when you gaze at the night sky, you must remember: *it is not the star sphere itself which is moving. The movement is due to the Earth spinning on its axis once every 24 hours and this makes it appear as if the stars revolve once in that time.*

Nevertheless, having said this, further observation from night to night will soon reveal that each star rises 4 minutes earlier than it did the previous night. Keeping watch on the stars week by week and month by month will show that the whole star sphere appears to shift round completely. This gradual shift, which is quite separate from the shift we notice over 24 hours, occurs because the Earth not only spins on its axis but also revolves round the Sun in a period of one year. This is the reason we see constellations change from season to season. Referring to the sky maps, we can see that constellations due south, north, east or west at any given time are different according to the season.

CONSTELLATIONS

In the night sky the stars are seen to form patterns, or groups, called constellations.

No one is sure who first made up star patterns to form constellations. The ones we know today date back at least 4,000 years to Babylonian times.

In about 280 BC, a Greek poet called Aratus of Soli wrote some verses about constellations, and these are the oldest descriptions of them in existence. The earliest pictures of constellations are engraved on a Roman sculpture known as the Atlante Farnese Globe, now in a museum in Naples. The globe shows Atlas resting on one knee, and on the surface of the globe he carries above his head are pictures of 42 constellations as the Greeks saw them. Five others have been obliterated by the ravages of time.

The Chinese and the ancient Egyptians also had constellation pictures, as well as pictures for individual bright stars like Sirius. The Egyptian ones are recorded on the Dendera 'planisphere' now in a Paris museum. The Chinese and Egyptian pictures are mostly quite different from the Greek ones. Only a few of the Egyptian pictures can be identified because later Egyptian artists made mistakes in copying them from much older pictures which are now lost.

Key constellations

People who live in the northern hemisphere are luckier than those who live in the southern because several constellations in the northern skies have very distinct, easy to recognise shapes. Once these are identified it makes the less distinctive ones near by easy to spot.

The most prominent constellation in the northern sky is called the Great Bear, or Ursa Major, which is simply the Latin name for Great Bear. The ancient sky-watchers had vivid imaginations and gave all the constellations, including the Zodiacal ones (p 11), either names of animals, familiar things or personages from mythology. Actually, to our eyes, the Great Bear does not look much like a bear except for the tail part. In North America it is also known as the Big Dipper, and an old English name for it was Charles's Wain (a wain is a cart).

To find it, first look for it on the star maps and then go outdoors on a clear, moonless night. Let your eyes get used to the darkness. This will take three or four minutes. Face north and, depending on the time of year and time of night, carefully search out the seven stars which form this constellation. In autumn, in early evening, Ursa Major will be low down looking like a saucepan with a bent handle, but in spring it will be above your head 'upside down' and then its shape is slightly more difficult to trace. At other times it will be tilted.

The two stars farthest from the bent handle are called the Pointers because a line drawn through them and projected onwards about five times this distance finds the Pole Star, or Polaris. Once you can recognise the Great Bear and get to know its seasonal movements, you can always find true north at night. But remember, in or near cities, lights and smoke blot out the less bright stars so that it will be possible to see only the stars forming the more prominent constellations.

Using Ursa Major as a starting-point, together with the star maps, all the other constellations will fall into place. In winter skies, facing south, the constellation of Orion, the Hunter, is one of the easiest to spot. The three stars forming 'the Sword Belt of the Hunter' act as a pointer eastwards and downwards towards Sirius which is the brightest star in the sky.

▲The ancient sky-watchers divided the stars into groups called constellations which often took the form of familiar animals such as the Bear, the Lion, the Crab, etc. These figures appeared on star maps up to modern times. In this 17th-century example it is quite easy to pick out many of the traditional animals on the globe **opposite**.

Observing the constellations

Orion is a fascinating constellation full of naked-eye objects. Betelgeuse, forming 'the right shoulder of the hunter', is a very distinctive reddish star of a kind known as a red giant. It is the twelfth brightest star in the sky and much bigger than our Sun – its diameter is three times as large. It is also a variable star, and its brightness varies between magnitudes 0.3 and 1.1 (see p 40). Another bright star of the same reddish colour type is Aldebaran in the nearby constellation of Taurus, the Bull.

Rigel, in contrast to Betelgeuse and Aldebaran, is a very bluish-white hot star. One of the real jewels of the sky is the famous Great Nebula in Orion positioned just below Orion's three belt stars. With the unaided eye it looks like a misty blob, but through binoculars it is clearly visible as a greenish-coloured cloud. The nebula, or neb for short, belongs to the Milky Way and is a region where new stars are forming.

Another misty blob to the unaided eye lies in the constellation of Andromeda, the Chained Lady. This, one of the galaxies nearest our own Milky Way, is over two million light-years from us.

When you are outdoors looking at these objects, you will soon discover that staring slightly to one side of them gives you a better view. This is because the edges of the eyes' pupils are more sensitive to faint light than the middle.

Star names

Like the constellations, many of the brighter stars have names. Most of these were invented by the Greeks and the Arabs. Sirius is Greek for 'sparkling' or 'burning' while Betelgeuse comes from the Arabic – 'the Armpit of the Central One'. Rigel, another Arabic name, means 'Left Leg of the Giant'.

While astronomers still use these names, they really prefer to use a more scientific system invented in 1603 by the German astronomer Johann Bayer (1572–1625). Bayer labelled the stars in each separate constellation using Greek letters starting with the brightest: α (Alpha), β (Beta), γ (Gamma), and so on. In this system Sirius is α Canis Majoris, Betelgeuse α Orionis, Rigel β Orionis.

Of course, Greek letters are limited,

▼These four diagrams show the night sky at different times throughout the seasons. They are simpler versions of the large diagram opposite. From top left to bottom right, they show the sky in spring, summer, autumn and winter.

▶This chart shows stars visible from the Northern hemisphere (some faint stars are not shown). Each coloured oval 'window' shows the sky at midnight in a particular month. If you want to find the stars for December, find that oval. To see the stars in the south, turn the page so that the edge of the window marked **S** is at the bottom as you look at it. The bright star, Sirius, is to your left, or east. To see the stars in the east, turn the chart so the edge of the same window marked **E** is at the bottom, and so on.

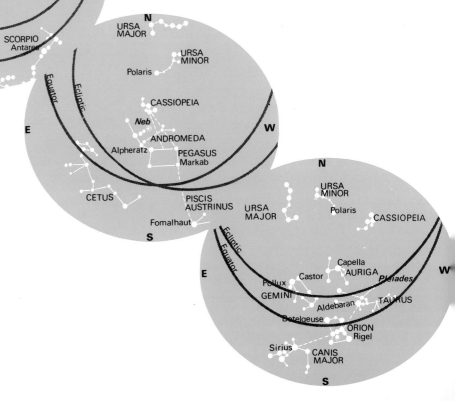

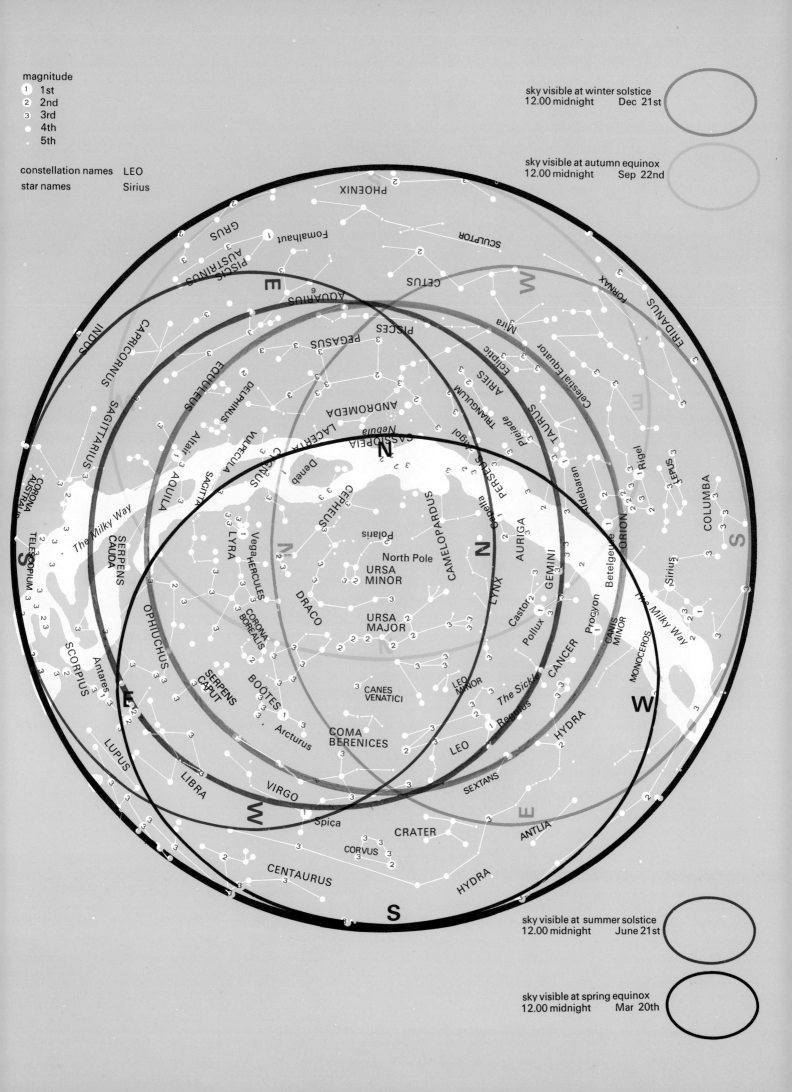

magnitude
1 1st
2 2nd
3 3rd
● 4th
· 5th

constellation names   LEO
star names   Sirius

sky visible at winter solstice
12.00 midnight   Dec 21st

sky visible at autumn equinox
12.00 midnight   Sep 22nd

sky visible at summer solstice
12.00 midnight   June 21st

sky visible at spring equinox
12.00 midnight   Mar 20th

and as more stars were discovered, astronomers had to devise additional systems of labelling them.

Brightness of stars and planets

Even a casual look at the night sky shows that the stars and planets differ in brightness. These differences are caused by two things. Firstly how big and bright they are and, in the case of stars, whether they are giants, average-sized or dwarfs. Secondly, how far the star or planet is from the Earth. Of two similar-sized and similar-coloured stars (or planets) the one closest will seem brightest.

The Greek astronomer Hipparchus (160–125 BC) divided the visible stars into six grades of brightness. The very brightest he called 1st-magnitude stars, the next brightest 2nd-magnitude stars and so on to the faintest he could see which he called 6th-magnitude stars.

Since Hipparchus's time the magnitude system has changed. The very brightest stars like Sirius and some others have minus (−) magnitudes to show they are really bright. For example, Sirius, the brightest visible star, has a magnitude of −1.4. The planet Venus can outshine Sirius and, seen at its brightest, reaches magnitude −4.4. On this same brightness scale the magnitude of the Moon is −12.7 while that of the sun −26.7, but usually magnitude is only used about stars, planets, comets, star clusters and galaxies. In astronomy the term magnitude is often shortened to mag.

With the naked eye we can see stars as faint as mag 6, just as Hipparchus did. If counted, all the visible stars on a clear, moonless night number about 3,000. Through ordinary binoculars you can see stars as faint as mag 9. If you have the patience to count them, there are about 200,000. The 508-cm (200-in) telescope at Mount Palomar (p 57) can photograph stars as faint as mag 23 and, if equipped with special devices, even fainter magnitudes.

The distances of stars

Until the 19th century no one knew how far away even the nearest stars were. Then in the 1830s and 1840s a method was devised to measure their distances.

THE NEAREST STARS		
Star	Apparent Magnitude	Distance (light years)
Proxima Centauri	10.7	4.2
α Centauri A	0.0	4.2
α Centauri B	1.4	4.3
Barnard's Star	9.5	5.9
Wolf 359	13.7	7.6
Lalande 21185	7.5	8.1
Sirius A	−1.4	8.7
Sirius B w	8.7	8.7
Luyten 726–8 A	12.4	8.7
Ross 154	10.6	9.3
Ross 248	12.3	10.3
ε Eridani	3.7	10.7
Ross 128	11.1	10.9
Luyten 789–6	12.6	11.0
61 Cygni A	5.2	11.2
61 Cygni B	6.0	11.2
Procyon A	0.5	11.4
Procyon B w	10.8	11.4
ε Indi	4.7	11.4
Struve 2398 A	8.9	11.5
w = white dwarf		

Astronomers were astounded to discover the nearest one was so far away from the Earth that it takes light travelling at a speed of about 300,000 km (186,000 miles) per second *just over 4.2 years* to reach us – a journey of about 39,900,000,000,000 km (25,200,000,000,000 miles).

Because it is impractical to write down such large numbers, astronomers express stellar distances in light-years. One light-year equals about 9,500,000,000,000 km (6,000,000,000,000 miles).

The spectrum

Isaac Newton discovered that when he passed a beam of sunlight through a wedge-shaped piece of glass called a prism, it was split into various colours as occurs when we see a rainbow (p 55).

Later astronomers found that these colours of sunlight – red, orange, yellow, green, blue, indigo and violet – contained mysterious dark lines called absorption lines, or bands, which are the tell-tale chemical prints of iron, copper, hydrogen, etc. that make up the Sun and other bodies. By carefully mapping the lines, or bands, and noting what lines occurred in the various colours, it was possible to obtain a great deal of information about the Sun and other bodies (p 48).

After light has been split into its seven colours, it is known as a *spectrum*, from Latin 'to see'. The study of the colours of light is called *spectroscopy*, and the instrument used to do this is called a *spectroscope*.

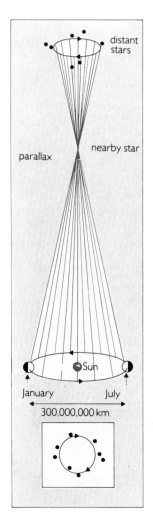

▼Not until the 1830s did astronomers discover how far away the stars were. To do this they used the diameter of the Earth's orbit round the Sun 300,000,000 km (186,411,360 miles) as a kind of surveyor's base line. They then observed a star at six monthly intervals (January and July). In that time the star would appear to move slightly against the background of more distant stars. From this they could find a star's *parallax* – its amount of shift. Once they knew this it was easy to work out the distance using trigonometry.

distant stars

parallax

nearby star

Sun

January   July

300,000,000 km

STARS

Even the nearest stars are so far away we are unable to view their surface regions as we can the Sun's. No matter how large a telescope or how much magnification is applied, the stars remain distant twinkling points. Nevertheless, by using special methods and instruments, astronomers are able to measure the diameters and temperatures of many stars – as well as their distances and, using the spectroscope, find what they are made of.

Among the stars in our own galaxy, and the galaxies beyond it, are a great variety of objects varying in size and temperature. Some giant stars have diameters more than 1,000 times that of our Sun (diameter 1,392,000 km or 865,000 miles). Others are dwarfs no larger than the planets in our own solar system and shine so dimly that even those near to us are very faint or invisible in ordinary telescopes.

Astronomers classify stars by their various qualities. There are white, red and black dwarfs; subgiants; giants; supergiants and 'average' stars like our Sun. Another means of classifying stars is by their colour – or temperature – because the colour of a star is usually a sure guide to how hot it is, how it is burning up its stock of nuclear fuel and its life history so far. Stars, like humans, are born, evolve through various stages, grow old and then finally die.

The hottest stars shine with a greenish-white light and have surface temperatures of over 40,000°C. These are followed in descending order of temperature by stars which are blue-white, white, yellowish-white, yellow (like the Sun whose surface glows at 6,000°C), yellow-orange, orange-red and the coolest of *visible* stars, deep red. There are even cooler stars which shine only in infra-red light. X-ray stars are even more mysterious objects, and there are probably other peculiar stars still unknown.

Everything basic that has ever been made in the universe has been made inside stars. Even the iron in our red blood-cells was made inside them.

Double stars

Many stars that appear single to the naked eye are found to be double (or even more than two) when examined through a telescope.

There are two kinds of double star: true doubles known as *binaries* (from Latin for 'two') which revolve together, and *optical pairs* which appear double in telescopes simply because one star lies in the same line of view as we see them from Earth. Some of the stars in optical pairs may, in fact, be separated in space by hundreds of light-years.

Some binaries are so close they cannot be seen as separate points even in the largest telescopes. If that is the case how do astronomers know these really are double stars?

The answer lies in the spectroscope (p 40). It was discovered that sometimes the dark lines, or bands, seen in the spectra (plural of spectrum) of starlight were all double. The only explanation could be that there must be two stars shining very close together – too close to tell apart with a telescope but quite easy for astronomers to do using the spectroscope. By measuring the positions and the slight movements of these double lines, and working on the basic laws first discovered by Kepler and Newton, astronomers can calculate the orbits of these unseen double stars. It is also possible to find out how big and how hot they are.

Some binary systems have more than two stars, and it must be a remarkable sight for anyone on a planet nearby to see the variously coloured suns all shining and revolving in the sky at the same time.

Variable stars

Not all stars shine with a constant brightness. Some may vary their light over a few hours, others over a year or more. Some have variations as precise as a clock, others are extremely irregular.

Variable stars are divided into about five main types. Some, however, are not true variables. They are spectroscopic binary pairs and only vary in brightness

Some double stars are easy to spot among the constellations. Perhaps the easiest one is Mizar, the second star 'along the handle' in Ursa Major (where the bend is). Its 4th mag companion star can easily be spotted. The Arabs named it Alcor and thought seeing it was a test for good eyesight. Mizar and Alcor were sometimes known as 'the Horse and his Rider'. In a telescope, Mizar has a much closer companion, which was also the first spectroscopic binary system to be discovered.

►Algol in the constellation of Perseus is a variable star which varies its brightness because one star passes in front of the other – or eclipses it. Two stars revolve in just under 3 days, and during that time the light varies in magnitude (brightness) from 2.2 to 3.5. Its variation can be detected with the naked eye if you watch carefully at the correct times. In panel **1** Algol's brightness remains constant. **2** The brightness drops as the larger star partially eclipses the smaller one. **3** There is also a small dip in brightness when the smaller star partially eclipses the larger one. The large dip in brightness takes about 5 hours and then 5 hours later the normal brightness is regained.

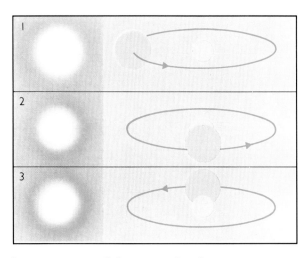

because one of the stars in the system gets in front of the other – or eclipses it as the Moon eclipses the Sun. The most famous variable star of this type is Algol, named 'the Demon' by the Arabs who discovered it long ago.

Other varieties of variable star pulsate and expand and then contract in a regular rhythm. Others are not so regular, for example, the red giant star Betelgeuse in Orion or Mira in the constellation of Cetus, the Whale (see large star map on p 39).

▼Radio telescopes have recording devices so that incoming signals can be recorded on a paper trace. This trace shows that the strong pulse (tall peak) of a pulsar is picked up every 24 milliseconds (thousandths of a second). Such pulses might come from a pulsar in position **b** on the **right**. In **a** the lefthand pulses disappear into space.

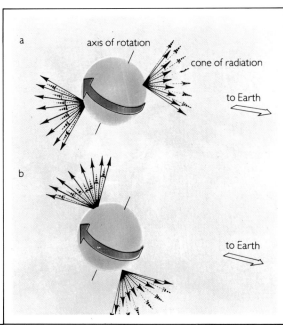

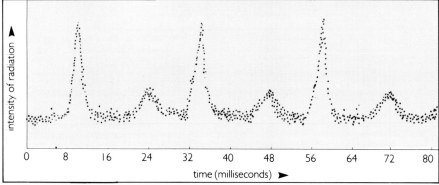

Among the most interesting variables are those called novae (Latin for 'new'). These are sometimes called temporary, or exploding stars. In spite of the name 'new', they are not newly born but are stars which have previously shone more faintly and then for some reason suddenly flare up, or explode, scattering their debris far and wide. Some of them are called supernovae and are more brilliant than the ordinary variety. One of these supernovae was seen by Tycho Brahe in Cassiopeia in 1572 and was visible in daylight. Another occurred in 1054 in Taurus. This later became the famous Crab Nebula where, in recent times, a new variety of star called a pulsar was discovered.

Pulsars
Pulsars are a new variety of star first discovered in 1967 with a radio telescope at Cambridge, England. They rotate very rapidly and send out flashes, or pulses, of radiation like lighthouses in space. Most pulsars, however, flash much faster. One called 4C21.53 (its number in the fourth Cambridge Catalogue of Radio Sources) rotates 642 times per second. This peculiar star is only about 10 km (6 miles) in diameter and spins so rapidly its equator moves at a speed of 40,000 km (25,000 miles) per second. It is made of material so dense that its surface gravity is a million million million times that on Earth.

Astronomers believe pulsars are old dwarf stars in the final stages of their lives and they are dying because their nuclear furnaces are almost burnt out. Most are only detected on radio waves, but some are visible in optical telescopes. One pulsar like this was spotted in 1969 in the Crab Nebula (M 1) and is linked to a supernova explosion seen by Chinese and Korean sky-watchers in AD 1054 in the constellation of Taurus, the Bull.

When radio waves from the first pulsar were detected, astronomers were greatly puzzled by them. One interesting idea was that they might be signals from other intelligent civilisations. Until astronomers at Cambridge found out what they were, they jokingly nicknamed them Little Green Men – source 1! Soon,

however, it was realised they were radio waves from a new kind of star. Since then many other pulsars have been discovered.

Globular star clusters

Some of the most impressive objects in the Milky Way are vast collections of stars clustered together in the shape of a globular mass. Such groups have therefore been called globular clusters. They are situated at great distances from the Sun, the nearest is about 20,000 light-years away. In the northern skies the Great Cluster in Hercules – which lies at the western side of the distinctive 'flower-pot' shape of stars in Hercules – appears in small binoculars as a faint patch of light. In long-exposure photographs, taken with large telescopes, thousands of individual stars are seen. In the southern skies an even brighter cluster is plainly visible to the naked eye, shining as a star in the constellation of Centaurus.

Open star clusters

In contrast to the densely packed stars found in globular clusters, open clusters are groups of stars with little or no compactness in their centres. Usually they consist of a few hundred members or often less, arranged quite haphazardly. One of the best known is the Pleiades Cluster, called 'the Seven Sisters', in which six members are plainly visible to the unaided eye, although many more can be seen through binoculars. You can find the Pleiades by starting at Orion's three belt stars and projecting a line upwards to the right (west) beyond the bright star Aldebaran.

◄The first pulsar to be seen in an optical telescope was found in the Crab Nebula (seen here), so called because in the 19th century it looked crab-like in large telescopes. Many pulsars are not visible in ordinary light and can only be detected by the radio waves they broadcast into space as they spin rapidly. These radio waves are believed to come from two points on the dying star (see left). Because of this, from Earth, we might only see one point – depending on how the waves are directed into space from the pulsar.

◄This globular cluster of stars, known as the Great Cluster in Hercules, is one of the finest in the sky and consists of perhaps 100,000 stars. Another name for it is M 13. In the 18th century a Frenchman called Charles Messier made a catalogue of star clusters and nebulae, and this was number 13 on his list – hence M 13.

▲The ancient sky-watchers called the Pleiades 'the Seven Sisters'; they were supposed to be the seven daughters of Atlas. Their names were Alcyone, Merope, Maya, Electra, Taygete, Sterope and Celaeno. Legend says that Merope was the only sister who married a mortal, and this is why she is fainter than her sisters. Indeed, most people will only be able to see six stars with the naked eye. The Australian Aborigines believed this group of stars to be more important than the Sun and to influence the weather. It is located in the constellation of Taurus the Bull. Mixed in among these stars, and seen in this photograph, is hot gas and dust.

NEBULAE

Nebulae (singular nebula) – from Latin for 'cloud' or 'mist' – was the name given by sky-watchers in the 17th and 18th centuries to patches of faint light they observed among the stars. In more recent times, and with better telescopes available, astronomers found that some of these nebulae were really star clusters, or distant galaxies far beyond the Milky Way, so the name is wrongly applied in these instances. Nevertheless, the word 'nebula' is still widely, if loosely, used about such objects.

However, scattered among the stars of the Milky Way are true nebulae composed of cloud-like wisps of luminous gas and dust, often very irregular in shape. Some have highly individual forms and are nicknamed according to the shape they suggested – hence the North America Nebula, the Veil Nebula and the Trifid (from the Greek 'three-cleft'). Another famous nebula is the Crab, so called because it looked like a crab in large telescopes used in the 19th century, but it does not appear very crab-like in modern photographs.

▼The Trifid Nebula is a large cloud of gas and dust inside our own Milky Way where new stars are probably being formed.

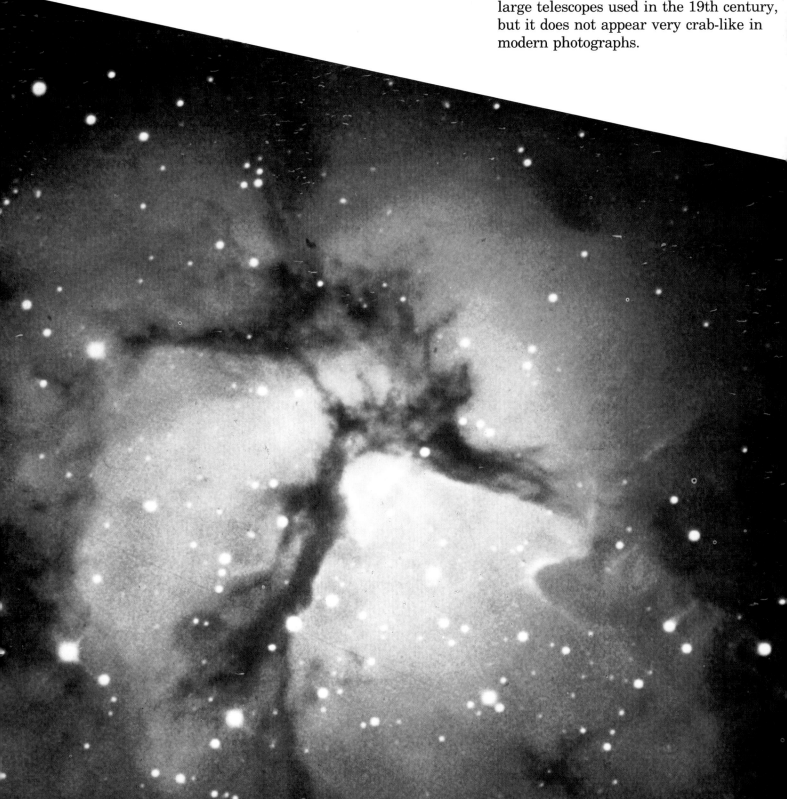

▲This photograph shows the distinct shapes of the North America Nebula (upper left) and the Veil Nebula (lower left). The Veil Nebula is a remnant of a supernova explosion which took place thousands of years ago and is part of the shell of gas blown out by the exploding star which is still expanding outwards.

45

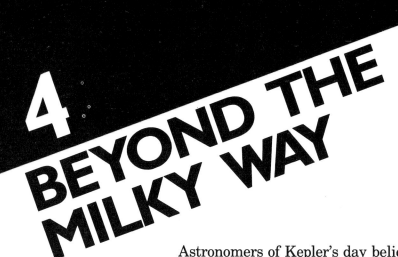

4 BEYOND THE MILKY WAY

Astronomers of Kepler's day believed the Sun was the centre of the universe, but when men of the 17th and 18th centuries began to catalogue the different objects they saw, they soon realised this idea was incorrect. One of these catalogues was made by the Frenchman Charles Messier (1730–1817) who listed all the nebulous objects he could find in his hunt for comets – at first glance the two objects can be confused in small telescopes. Many of the larger nebulae, galaxies and clusters are still known by their Messier, or M, numbers, eg M 31 is the Great Nebula in Andromeda.

The work of the Herschels
Later, another hunter of the nebulae was William Herschel, already famous for his discovery of the planet Uranus. With his equally famous sister Caroline (1750–1848) to help record their observations, they spent long nights outdoors making the first detailed survey of the size of the universe.

Herschel discovered many new faint nebulae. Through his larger telescopes he noted some had distinctive shapes which intrigued him. Might not these be remote independent systems of stars, 'island universes' in their own right? However, he realised some other nebulae, like the irregular-shaped ones (which we now know are made of gas and dust) were different again and perhaps by comparison were not that far away. But how far away any nebulae were, no one at that time could tell.

After Herschel's death, his son, John (1792–1871), continued this work of surveying the heavens. In 1833 he took his family, and a large telescope he had made earlier under his father's directions, to South Africa. He stayed there until 1838, surveying nebulae in the southern skies which his father had not been able to see from the northern hemisphere.

Between them the Herschels discovered thousands of new nebulae, but although other astronomers were by now also guessing that some of them were indeed remote objects, no one could think of a way to measure their distances.

Another telescope – bigger than that used by the Herschels – came into use in 1845. This was the Earl of Rosse's 184-cm (72-in) monster located in Ireland. Some of the nebulae viewed through it were clearly seen to have whirlpool, or spiral, forms – showing they were probably rotating slowly.

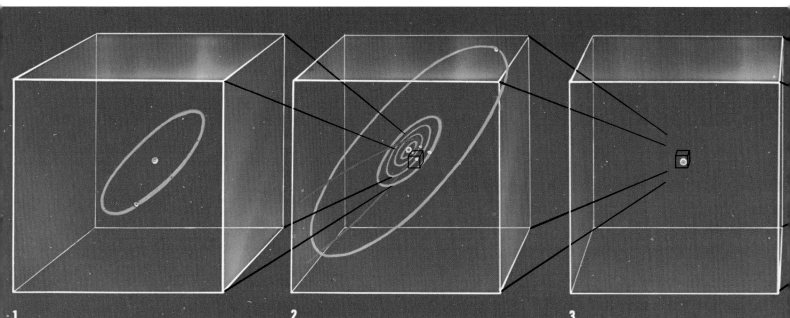

1 2 3

THE DEPTHS OF SPACE

No one knew how far away the 'whirlpool' type nebulae were until after World War I when the new 254-cm (100-in) reflecting telescope was first used at Mount Wilson in California. The light-collecting power of this telescope was so great that astronomers could now take photographs of very faint objects. Not long after, two American astronomers, Edwin Powell Hubble (1889–1953) and Milton Humason, discovered the answer to the distance of the 'whirlpools'.

To do this the two Americans used known facts about a class of variable star called a Cepheid (pronounced 'sefid' or 'sefeid') which occurs in the Milky Way. Astronomers had worked out the distance of Cepheid variables from Earth. Using the extra-powerful Mount Wilson telescope, new Cepheid variables were identified in distant nebulae. By noting how these compared with the ones already known, the newly discovered Cepheids provided an astonishing answer: they were almost *one million light-years away*! Herschel's old idea was proved right. Some of the nebulae were 'island universes' in their own right – galaxies lying far beyond the borders of our own Milky Way.

Unfortunately the basic information about Cepheid variables was later found to be wrong. However, when this was corrected, another surprise was in store.

It showed the distant galaxies were *twice* as far away as first calculated by Hubble!

'Near' neighbours in space

As far as we can see in space there are galaxies in huge numbers often swarming in great clusters. The Milky Way itself belongs to a cluster of galaxies called the local group.

Two members of this local group are known as the Greater Magellanic Cloud and the Lesser Magellanic Cloud – after the Portuguese navigator Ferdinand Magellan, who sailed round the world in 1519. The Latin names for these galaxies are Nubecula Major and Nubecula Minor. Both Magellanic clouds are irregular-shaped galaxies and are much smaller and closer to us than the Andromeda spiral. They lie about 150,000 light-years away. Some astronomers think they are satellite galaxies of the Milky Way and may have broken off in remote times. They are plainly visible to the naked eye in the southern hemisphere.

Since the Magellanic clouds can be seen from the Cape of Good Hope in South Africa, they are often called 'the Cape Clouds'. In Australia, in the last century, they were called 'the Drover's Friends' because they were used as directional aids when cattle were moved during the cool of night. The Polynesians also used them as navigational 'beacons' when they sailed between islands.

▼The various cubes show the vast scale of the universe. The first cube is about a million miles across, then each following cube is a region a thousand times wider than the one before.
1 The Earth is circled by the Moon, about 250 thousand miles away.
2 The orbits of the 5 inner planets lie within 500 million miles of the Sun, but a comet (red orbit) may travel far out beyond the normal frontiers of the solar system...
3 Within half a million million miles of the Sun, or about one twelfth of a light-year, there are no stars as far as we know, and, except for wandering comets, space is empty.
4 Within 85 light-years of the Sun there are many stars. Some may have planets circling them...
5 The Sun lies about two thirds out from the centre of the Milky Way which is 100,000 light-years across...
6 Within 100 million light-years of our galaxy we see thousands of other galaxies, but these are only a fraction of all those in the universe.

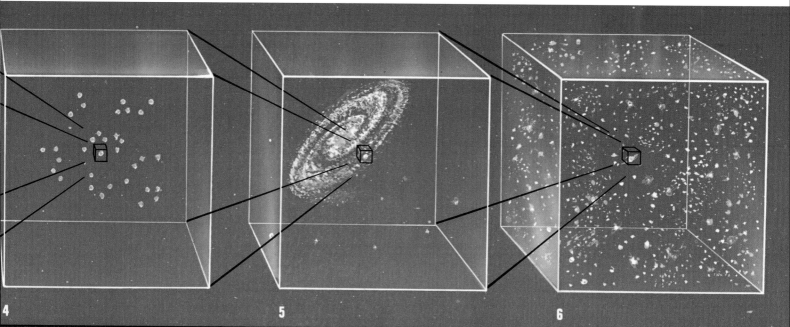

THE EXPANDING UNIVERSE

Some time before Hubble and Humason photographed the galaxies, another American astronomer, Vesto Melvin Slipher (1875–1969) photographed the Andromeda Nebula using a spectroscope.

He noticed the dark lines occurring in the various colours were shifted slightly towards one side. Astronomers knew by this time that a moving object when viewed with a spectroscope could produce this effect. If an object was moving *towards* us, the spectral lines were shifted towards the *violet end*, and if an object was moving *away* from us, they were shifted towards the *red end* of the spectrum.

The spectrum of the Andromeda Nebula showed it was approaching us, but Slipher did not then know its distance and so he had no way of telling how fast it was moving. Hubble and Humason continued this work, using the Mount Wilson telescope, and discovered a curious thing. The Andromeda spiral was the only one approaching us. The rest of the galaxies they photographed were all rushing away from us at high speed. Yet another curious thing was that the fainter the galaxy photographed, the greater was the shift of the lines towards the red end – now known as the red shift. Because Hubble and Humason now knew the distance of the galaxies, they were also able to compute the speed at which they were receding. Some were found to be rushing away at speeds of over 40,000 km (25,000 miles) per second. This led Hubble to coin the new expression: the expanding universe.

Since Hubble's time even greater recessional speeds have been measured in distant galaxies, and most astronomers support the idea of a continuously expanding universe.

ellipticals

spirals

barred spirals

▲Hubble classified galaxies into three main types: ellipticals, spirals and barred spirals. No one is sure which is the oldest type, but one theory suggests that galaxies are born as barred spirals or spirals and then evolve into ellipticals. Galaxies with no distinct shape are called irregulars.

▶The spiral galaxy numbered 51 in Messier's catalogue (M 51) lies in the direction of the constellation of Canes Venatici, the Hunting Dogs. It was one of the first nebulae to be seen in its true spiral form and was nicknamed 'the Whirlpool Nebula'.

▲An elliptical galaxy lying in the direction of Cassiopeia. Because elliptical galaxies are rich in old reddish stars and only have a little gas and dust, they may be the oldest type of galaxy.

QUASARS

Another modern discovery are quasars – short for quasi-stellar (star-like) radio sources. Some had long been visible through optical telescopes, but astronomers thought they were ordinary stars. When big radio telescopes came into service, they picked up signals that were identified with star-like objects already known from older photographs.

Because of their powerful radio sources, quasars were a puzzle and in many ways still are. When their spectra were photographed with large telescopes, they seemed to make little sense. Then, in 1963, Maarten Schmidt, a Dutch astronomer working at Mount Palomar, photographed a quasar spectrum and suddenly realised he was looking at a red shift far greater than anything he had seen before. If this large red shift was due to the same causes as Hubble's earlier research had shown – that the faintest objects had the biggest red shifts and therefore the largest recessional speeds – quasars were truly amazing objects, and some were apparently receding at near the speed of light, 300,000 km (186,000 miles) per second!

Although quasars apparently shine like very distant, faint stars, they must be hundreds of times brighter than entire galaxies, even though their radiations come from regions less than one light-year across. (Our own Milky Way is about 100,000 light-years across.) Because of this startling evidence, some astronomers refuse to believe that quasars are very distant objects. Perhaps Hubble's ideas about red shifts in galaxies are wrong. Some think that the huge displacements (shifts) of spectral lines in distant quasars may be caused by something else – gravity perhaps? Or, alternatively, quasars may be closer objects, thrown out of our Milky Way at high speeds by causes yet unknown. While most astronomers believe quasars are very distant objects receding at great speeds, no one yet can be absolutely certain.

◀This photograph of a quasar called 3C-273 was taken with the 500-cm (200-in) telescope at Mount Palomar, California. It was discovered in 1963 and lies in the direction of the constellation of Virgo and has a mysterious spike of material shooting out to one side of it. It is classified as 3C-273 in the 3rd Cambridge Catalogue of Radio Sources.

distance light years		speed km/sec
1,000 million		18,000
quasar A 2,000 million		36,000
quasar B 5,000 million		90,000
quasar C 7,000 million		126,000
quasar D 10,000 million		180,000

◀The spectra of four quasars show different red shifts of their dark lines which occur among the various colours. How much they are red-shifted depends on their distances and velocities of recession. The more distant ones have their dark spectral lines shifted from the green into the yellow and the very fastest receding ones even into the red.

ORIGIN OF THE UNIVERSE

If all the galaxies are rushing away at great speed, where were they in the past? All clustered together in a dense bunch? And why, with the exception of some of the nearer ones like the Andromeda spiral, are they rushing away?

Several theories have been put forward to answer these questions. One is that ten or more thousand million years ago, the present universe was born out of a 'Big Bang', and since then, as a result of the explosion, galaxies have been hurtling farther and farther into space.

But what caused the Big Bang? Was there another universe before this which had grown old and collapsed inwards as we know old stars do? No one really knows, but the Big Bang is the one idea that most astronomers favour because of the evidence provided by receding galaxies.

Another theory is the 'Steady State'.

◀The Great Nebula in Andromeda (M 31) is one of the nearer spiral galaxies to our own Milky Way. Even so it is over 2 million light-years away. It is thought our Milky Way looks something like this from outside. All the foreground stars in the photograph belong to the Milky Way, but the two larger blobs are other galaxies. On a clear, moonless night the Andromeda spiral can be seen with the naked eye as a faint misty patch.

This suggests the universe will go on expanding for ever and that new material is created all the time to fill the gaps.

Yet another idea, the 'Oscillating' theory, holds that one day the expanding universe will stop expanding and start to contract inwards. Then at a critical stage it will stop contracting and start to expand again. Such a universe would continue to expand and contract in a cyclic rhythm.

▼No-one knows how the universe began, but these diagrams show three of the theories. Astronomers hope that one day evidence will be found that shows exactly which is correct, or if the universe started in another way.

If the universe did begin with a 'Big Bang', and all the galaxies were born out of this, far out in space there should be a boundary where the most distant galaxies have receded to so far. At present, in telescopes, the universe shows no end. If space is curved and closed as Einstein believed it to be, light will bend back on itself and we shall never see 'outside'.

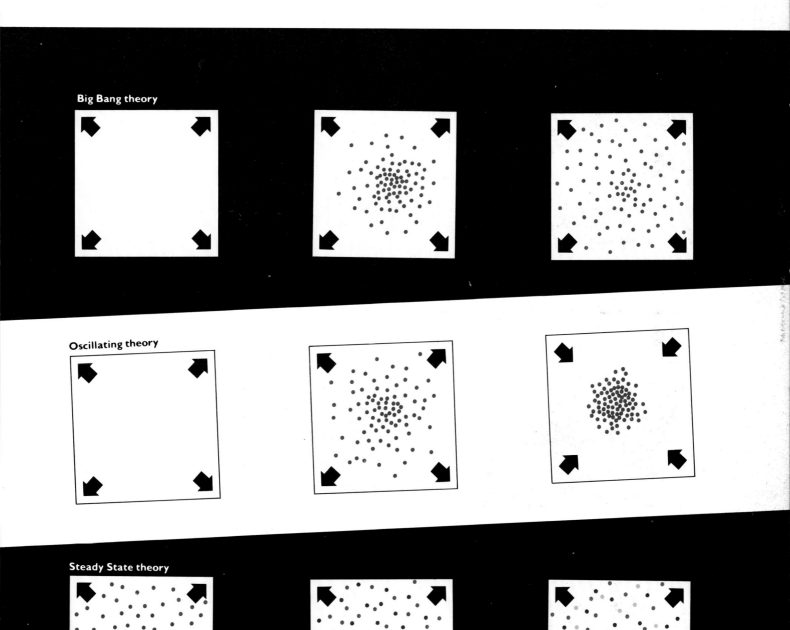

Big Bang theory

Oscillating theory

Steady State theory

5 TELESCOPES AND OBSERVATORIES

The human eye is one of the most sensitive optical instruments ever invented by nature and can detect a single bit (photon) of light. Nevertheless, as a *collector* of light it performs very poorly. Even a toy telescope will gather in its lens 150 times more light than the tiny lenses in our eyes.

Owing to this limitation of how far we can see out into space, our knowledge of the universe beyond naked-eye visibility was restricted until someone quite accidentally invented a light-collecting device – later called a telescope.

►In all telescopes light-rays are collected, focused then magnified. A refractor uses a glass lens (objective) at its front end and another (or several) to view the focused image at the eyepiece end. Galileo's telescopes were of this type, except the eyepiece lens was concave.

In 1668 Isaac Newton invented the reflecting telescope in which light-rays are collected by a concave mirror and then focused back to a smaller flat mirror which projects the image sideways into the eyepiece.

In 1672 a Frenchman, N. Cassegrain, designed a telescope in which the light-rays are reflected back down the tube through a hole in the mirror. The coudé reflector invented by the Austrian-French astronomer M. Loewy in 1894, uses two mirrors to project the light into the eyepiece.

All the big reflecting telescopes are constructed to work as Newtonian/Cassegrain/ coudé instruments because in some observations one type is better than the other.

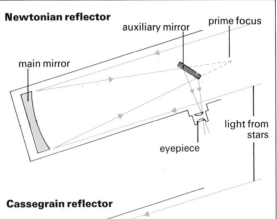

refractor

light from stars — objective lens — image — eyepiece

Newtonian reflector

main mirror — auxiliary mirror — prime focus — light from stars — eyepiece

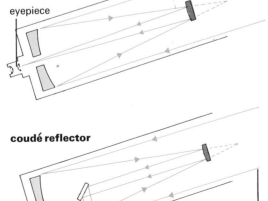

Cassegrain reflector

eyepiece

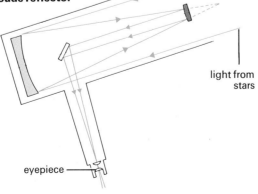

coudé reflector

light from stars — eyepiece

The first telescope

The word telescope comes from two Greek words *tele*, 'at a distance' and *scopein*, 'to observe'. No one knows for certain who invented the first telescope. According to one story a boy apprentice mischievously put one of his master's spectacle lenses in front of another and realised he could see a distant church steeple as if it were close up. Today, however, we believe that it was probably invented by Hans Lippershey, a Dutch spectacle-maker, in 1608. Perhaps the apprentice in the story worked for Lippershey and the master took all the credit!

Simple spectacle lenses had been known since ancient times. The Greeks are supposed to have set fire to enemy ships using huge lenses (or concave mirrors) as burning-glasses. The oldest known object that *looks* like a lens was found in an archaeological excavation in Babylonia and is thought to have been used as a magnifying glass to read inscriptions on clay tablets.

In Holland no one thought of looking at the heavens with the new invention. It was used as a military weapon because through it you could see the enemy before he saw you. In 1608 news and rumours about the wonderful new invention spread like wildfire through Europe. When Galileo heard about it, he also realised how useful it could be in time of war, but he thought of other possible uses as well. Even before one of the Dutch telescopes reached him in Italy, he had made one for himself.

The new heavens

Galileo's first telescope had an objective lens 4.2 cm (1.6 in) in diameter with a magnification of only ×3, but the one he made his astronomical discoveries with was longer with a lens 4.4 cm (1.75 in) in diameter and a magnification of ×33.

When he looked at the sky through this new instrument, he was like a new Columbus setting out on a voyage of discovery. Looking at the Milky Way, he realised that Democritus had been right in thinking it consisted of myriads of stars too far away to be seen separately. Through his *glass*, as the telescope was then called, Galileo saw a glitter of separate stars and much fainter ones that were invisible to the naked eye.

Galileo discovered craters and mountains on the Moon and spots on the Sun. In January 1610 he turned his telescope to Jupiter and immediately noticed three tiny pin-pricks of light lying almost in a straight line near the small yellow disk of the planet. Curious as to what they might be he watched them

night after night. Soon he noticed that the points shifted position, but they always stayed more or less in a straight line and always kept near Jupiter. Six days after his first observation he saw a fourth. Then he understood what he was looking at: Jupiter had four small bodies moving round it as the Moon moved round the Earth!

When Kepler heard the news, he called them *satellites*, from a Latin word *satellitis* for people who attach themselves to the rich and powerful in hope of gaining favours.

Others were also using telescopes to look at the heavens. A German astronomer, Simon Marius (1570–1624) obtained a Dutch glass and independently discovered the four satellites about the same time as Galileo. Galileo had called them 'the Medicean stars' to flatter one of the Medici princes of Italy. However, Marius called them Io, Europa, Ganymede and Callisto, after characters in Greek legends who had been connected with Jupiter. We still use these names, but they are also sometimes referred to as the Galilean Moons.

Next Galileo looked at Saturn. It was then the most distant planet known. He thought he saw through his telescope a tiny globe with a smaller globe positioned

Even a pair of old-fashioned opera glasses, or better still some modern binoculars, will let you 'discover' the four Galilean Moons of Jupiter for yourself.

The magnification of a telescope depends on the focal length of its object lens or mirror *divided* by the focal length of the eyepiece lens or lenses. For example, a refractor or reflector with a focal length of 152 cm (60 in) if used with an eyepiece of 2.5 cm (1 in) focal length gives a magnification of 60 or ×60. If the eyepiece were only 1.3 cm (½ in) in focal length (ie $\frac{60}{1}$), the magnification would be ×120; if the eyepiece were 5 cm (2 in) in focal length (ie $\frac{60}{2}$, the magnification would be ×30.

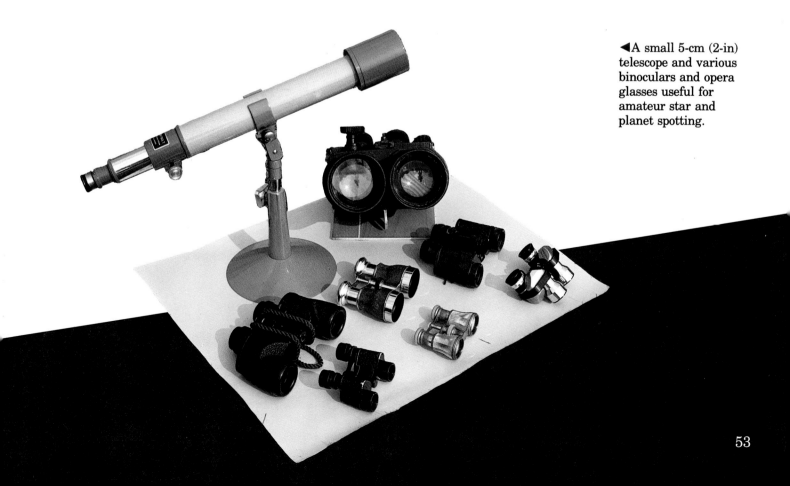

◄A small 5-cm (2-in) telescope and various binoculars and opera glasses useful for amateur star and planet spotting.

▶Galileo Galilei (**far right**) is the first person who we know used a telescope to study the heavens. His telescope (**right**) may look crude compared to those on pages 56 and 57, but it was immensely important for astronomy.

Galileo's telescopes which he made in 1609 were of the familiar spy-glass variety. This type is called a *refractor*. Such a telescope uses glass lenses. The front one – the light collector – is called the *object glass* (or objective) and this determines the size of the telescope. A 50-cm (2-in) telescope is one with an object glass 50 cm (2 in) in diameter.

The object glass collects incoming rays of light from the object under view and then bends (or refracts) them to form an image at the *focus* (where the light-rays come to a point). Another lens, or system of lenses, is used as an eyepiece to magnify the image.

Other types of optical telescopes are called *reflectors*. The first one was invented by Isaac Newton in about 1668. Instead of a lens this kind of telescope uses a *concave glass mirror* (with a coating of aluminium) to collect incoming light. The mirror lies at the bottom of a tube, and the incoming light it collects is then focused (bent) back up the tube to a small, flat mirror set at an angle of 45°. This secondary mirror projects the light-rays into an eyepiece made of glass lenses like the ones used in the refractor.

either side of the larger one – as if Saturn were made of three bodies in a line.

This puzzled him, but he continued to observe Saturn and by 1612 he noticed the two smaller globes had disappeared completely. Now he doubted his earlier observations and stopped looking at the planet.

Instead he turned his telescope to Venus and discovered that it showed a crescent shape. This he realised was proof that Copernicus was right when he said Venus went round the Sun and not the Earth.

Galileo's earlier problem with his observations of Saturn was due to poor-quality telescope lenses which distorted the image he saw. As a result his telescope was not able to show Saturn's famous ring *as a ring*. This discovery was not announced until 1656 when a Dutch astronomer, Christiaan Huygens (1629–

95), constructed a much better telescope than Galileo's.

When the two small bodies Galileo had earlier seen disappeared from either side of Saturn in 1612, he had not believed his own eyes. But this was an accurate observation. As seen from the Sun, Saturn's rings remain tilted in the same direction, but as seen from the Earth they appear to open and close over a period of time. For this reason the rings are occasionally seen tilted edge on to the Earth and because they are very thin, they become quite invisible even in the largest telescopes. The rings were tilted edge on in 1612 when Galileo observed Saturn.

Bigger and better telescopes
Following Galileo's first observations, telescopes were improved, and Kepler himself invented new ideas for lenses. In Galileo's telescopes the optical system showed the image the right way up as in opera glasses, binoculars and the small spotting telescopes used today for ordinary outdoor purposes. In astronomy, however, it does not matter which way up we see an object, and the inverted system invented by Kepler has several distinct advantages over the Galilean system. Today almost all astronomical telescope show the object 'upside down'.

In early (refractor) telescopes the object glasses often acted like prisms and caused rainbow colours to appear all round the edges of the object under view. This is called chromatic aberration. This was annoying, and to try and get over this difficulty, telescopes were made with very long focal lengths which helped reduce the amount of colour. The telescope Huygens used to discover the true nature of Saturn's rings, which had puzzled Galileo, was 37 m (123 ft) long and was a very cumbersome instrument to operate. Another astronomer built a telescope 65 m (212 ft) long.

In 1668 Isaac Newton invented an entirely new kind of telescope (a reflector), using a mirror instead of an object lens. This avoided the problem of colours because when a mirror focuses light, it does not split it into its primary colours.

However, for some kinds of observing the refractor was better than the reflector. The mirror used for Newton's telescope and later reflecting telescopes was made of a shiny metal called speculum which soon tarnished and needed frequent polishing and refiguring. The refractor was improved in 1733 when an Englishman, Chester Moor Hall (1703–71), invented a new kind of object glass called an *achromatic* which finally got rid of the colour nuisance.

William Herschel's telescopes
Refracting telescopes with the new type lenses were expensive. When William Herschel became interested in astronomy in the 1770s, he could not afford to buy a telescope so he purchased some cheap lenses of the old kind and put them inside a pasteboard tube to observe Jupiter. But he was dissatisfied with its performance. He asked someone to make him a mirror so he could build a reflector, but the price was too high. Then he read some books to find out how mirrors were made. With this knowledge he built his own reflector and tested it in what he called 'the lucid spot in Orion's sword belt' – the Great Nebula in Orion to us.

Herschel then built bigger and better telescopes. He discovered the planet Uranus with one on 13 March 1781, and he became famous overnight. Soon he was building the largest telescopes in the world to use in his searches for the nebulae. With one of his large telescopes he later discovered at least two of the satellites of Uranus.

His largest telescope was 122 cm (48 in) in diameter, but this was never quite as successful as some of his smaller ones. His 122-cm telescope remained the largest in the world until the Earl of Rosse built his 184-cm (72-in) monster at Birr Castle in Ireland in 1845. Through this telescope – nicknamed 'the Leviathan' – the spiral shapes of distant nebulae were first seen.

▼Isaac Newton showed that when light is passed through a glass prism, it will split it into its rainbow colours. Later astronomers discovered that these colours also contain dark lines which tell us what the chemical elements are in the source of light. In this way we are able to tell what chemical elements are contained in the Sun and other stars. Other kinds of light, like that from a discharge tube, or lamp, show bright line spectra instead of dark lines but these too are patterns due to particular elements in the source of light, and some stars have bright lines like these. Astronomers who examine spectra use an instrument called a spectroscope which is attached to the eyepiece end of a large telescope.

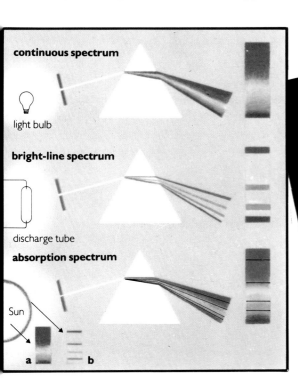

continuous spectrum
light bulb
bright-line spectrum
discharge tube
absorption spectrum
Sun
a   b

Modern telescopes

The Earl of Rosse's 184-cm (72-in) telescope was not a great success. It was fixed so that it could only see a limited part of the sky, and the large, heavy mirror of shiny speculum distorted under its own great weight, preventing the telescope from being used to observe fine details on planets.

In the middle of the 19th century it was discovered that silver could be deposited on glass and therefore glass could be used for mirrors instead of speculum. This revolutionised the design of reflecting telescopes, and they became cheaper to build than the conventional refracting telescopes using large lenses.

Today all large telescopes like the 508-cm (200-in) giant at Mount Palomar are reflectors. Special glass has replaced the older, ordinary glass, and a thin film of aluminium is now used to coat the mirrors.

OBSERVATORIES

Modern reflecting telescopes take several forms, but nearly all are based on the types first built in the 17th, 18th and 19th centuries. Herschel's and the Earl of Rosse's telescopes were out in the open and exposed to the weather. All modern telescopes are housed inside large domes which protect them and they have sliding

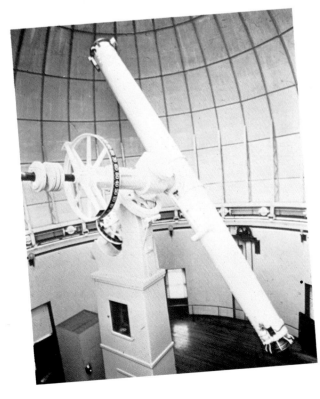

►This is the 65-cm (26-in) refracting telescope at the Washington Naval Observatory, USA. In 1877 it was used to discover the two tiny moons circling Mars.

shutters large enough, when opened, for the telescope to view the sky. They are also computer controlled and at the touch of a button the telescope can be adjusted to swing round to any part of the sky and then track on a celestial object for several hours while photographs are taken. Nearly all observations are photographic ones. Professional astronomers no longer sit with their eyes glued to the telescope as they did in the old days.

RADIO TELESCOPES

Just as all the great modern optical telescopes of today are direct descendants of Galileo's and Newton's crude pioneer instruments, the great radio telescopes also descend from the first crude radio telescope devised in 1932 by an American, Karl Jansky (1905–50).

Jansky accidentally discovered cosmic radio waves while working as an engineer for the Bell Telephone Company. The company wanted him to try to identify strange noises or 'static' which interfered with radio communications. To do this Jansky built an apparatus of wires like a merry-go-round so he could find which direction the strange noises came from. He knew that thunder and lightning caused noises, but those were always heard as crackling sounds. Yet as well as crackling there was a low and steady hissing noise which was always present.

Tracking its source became his obsession. He checked the Sun, but found the hissing sounds moved relative to the stars and not the Sun. The Sun does give off radio waves – especially at the time of the peak 11-year sunspot cycle – but Jansky was working at a time of sunspot minimum and at this time there was very little Sun noise. He directed his crude aerial all round the sky and checked the stars, constellation by constellation. Finally he found the source. It came from a spot in the Milky Way – the very spot in Sagittarius believed to be at the centre of our galaxy!

Since Jansky's time other great discoveries have been made. In many ways radio telescopes have surpassed the

►The 508-cm (200-in) reflector at Mount Palomar in California took many years to build. It can be used as either a Newtonian, Cassegrain or coudé telescope. The observer directs the telescope to any part of the sky by computer-button control. All large telescopes are now photographic instruments.

►In William Herschel's time astronomers observed under the open skies. Today huge domes protect telescopes, and a shutter is opened wide enough to allow a view of the galaxy or starfield being photographed. As the stars shift in the night sky, the telescope and the dome are driven round by a motor to follow them.

explorations made by optical telescopes because they can 'see' farther into space. With radio telescopes astronomers detected the peculiar nature of quasars and later discovered pulsars. In addition they have been used to map the sky in detail for the various kinds of radio signals emitted by stars, nebulae and galaxies. Radio telescopes are now huge and come in all shapes and sizes. However, they mainly consist of two types: dishes and linear arrays.

Dish radio telescopes

The dish type is the more familiar kind. It can be fixed or steerable. Unlike optical telescopes, the surface of radio telescopes need not be super-accurate. But just as an optical reflector collects light waves, the dish collects radio waves and focuses them into a radio receiver where they are magnified (amplified) and recorded in a nearby control room which is computer operated.

The diameter (aperture) of a radio telescope determines how far it can 'see' in space. The size of the dishes in movable radio telescopes is limited by material strengths because parts bend and twist in high winds. To overcome this problem, fixed dishes are sometimes used. Instead of pointing the dish to any part of the sky, the sky must rotate towards the telescope, so they are not as convenient to use as the steerable type.

◄The giant radio telescope at Cambridge, England, has two aerials – one 500 m (1,100 ft) long and the other nearly 60 m (200 ft) long. Mounted on railway track, it can be tilted or moved in a north–south direction. These aerials can detect nebulae 5,000 million light years away.

◄This dish radio telescope is at Effelburg in Germany. It can be steered to any part of the sky. Its surface consists of a mesh of wires, and radio waves are gathered and then focused (as in an optical telescope) to a point where they are magnified (amplified). Note its huge size in relation to the cars parked alongside it.

59

Linear radio telescopes

The second kind, the linear array, is also fixed. It consists of long lines of aerials arranged in different forms. Some are like a cross because this shape gives a much sharper 'picture' of a radio source.

Two radio telescopes can be used like one big one. Using a radio telescope at either end of a measured base line, they can work as if the base line were the actual diameter (aperture) of a telescope. If a radio telescope were carried to the Moon's surface and linked with a radio telescope back on Earth, it would make the biggest radio telescope yet made by man.

▲This is the linear array radio telescope at Medicina in Italy. The red-painted section is part of the north–south arm of the cross. This type of radio telescope was invented by Bernard Mills and all similar ones are called Mills Cross type telescopes.

SPACE OBSERVATORIES

Because the Earth's atmosphere restricts our view of the objects we see outside it, manned space observatories orbiting the Earth, and unmanned ones travelling to the planets, provide us with new information about the solar system.

The American Pioneer and Voyager probes have gone farthest. Pioneers 10 and 11 were launched in 1972 and 1973 to view Jupiter while Voyagers 1 and 2, launched in 1977, were sent to view the planets beyond. They have provided many new facts about Jupiter and Saturn. After passing on, Voyager 2 will explore Uranus in 1986, then Neptune.

When all these probes move on to the outer reaches of the planetary system, they will enter the domain of the comets and later still travel on towards the stars. If nothing goes wrong on their journeys, the Pioneer probes will take 30 million years to travel the distance to Aldebaran, a bright star lying in the line of the constellation of Taurus, the Bull. By that time, however, the star itself will have moved further round the Milky Way.

These space probes will remain wanderers in our own galaxy. They will probably still be wandering when the Sun, thousands of millions of years from now, begins to swell into a red giant and finally swallows up the Earth. These probes might be the only evidence that Planet Earth was once inhabited by intelligent beings.

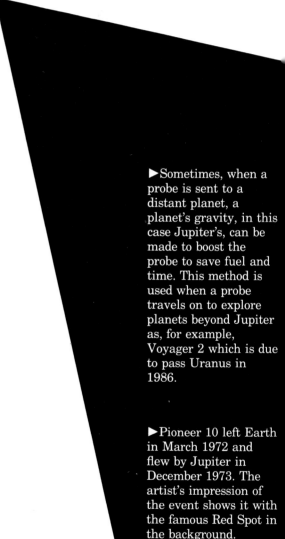

▶Sometimes, when a probe is sent to a distant planet, a planet's gravity, in this case Jupiter's, can be made to boost the probe to save fuel and time. This method is used when a probe travels on to explore planets beyond Jupiter as, for example, Voyager 2 which is due to pass Uranus in 1986.

▶Pioneer 10 left Earth in March 1972 and flew by Jupiter in December 1973. The artist's impression of the event shows it with the famous Red Spot in the background.

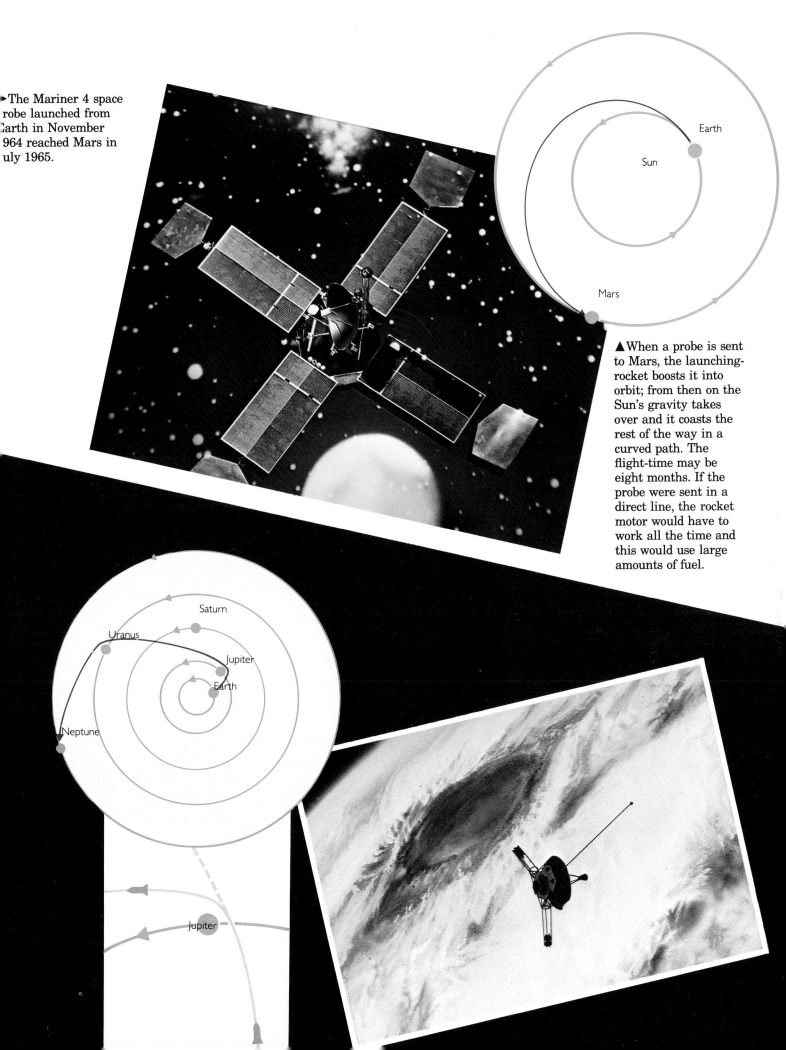

◄ The Mariner 4 space probe launched from Earth in November 1964 reached Mars in July 1965.

▲ When a probe is sent to Mars, the launching-rocket boosts it into orbit; from then on the Sun's gravity takes over and it coasts the rest of the way in a curved path. The flight-time may be eight months. If the probe were sent in a direct line, the rocket motor would have to work all the time and this would use large amounts of fuel.

GLOSSARY

Absorption lines are dark lines or bands occurring in the spectrum (see below) of a celestial body which enable astronomers to discover much about its chemical make-up.

Asteroid As well as the nine major planets in the solar system, there are thousands of tiny planets, or asteroids, mostly in orbit between Mars and Jupiter.

Atmosphere The envelope, or covering, of gases surrounding a star or planet.

Aurora occur in the skies above the Earth's sub-polar regions and are colourful atmospheric displays triggered by activity on the Sun – particularly at time of maximum sunspot activity.

Binary stars Some stars are part of a double, or binary (Latin for 'two') system, in which both members revolve in orbit round a common centre of gravity.

Black dwarf A variety of star which has grown old and is no longer visible in ordinary light. Such a star can only be detected by its gravitational pull on nearby bodies.

Cepheid A class of variable star which expands and then contracts (pulsates) in a regular almost clock-like rhythm. Cepheid variables can be used as yardsticks to measure the distance of galaxies.

Comet A comet is a curious cloud-like body which, like the planets, revolves round the Sun.

Constellation The name given to a group of stars forming a pattern.

Corona The outer part of the Sun's atmosphere that is visible as a pearly halo during a total eclipse of the Sun.

Eccentric orbit Sometimes the egg-shaped path (an ellipse, see below) of an asteroid or comet, as it journeys round the Sun, is very distorted, or eccentric.

Eclipse When one celestial body passes in front of another it is said to eclipse it.

Ecliptic The name given to the narrow path among the background stars over which the planets appear to travel as they journey round the Sun.

Ellipse The egg-shaped path traced out by a planet or comet as it journeys round the Sun.

Eon (or Aeon) A measure of time span (1 eon = 1,000,000,000 million years).

Galaxy The name given to our own Milky Way or to a very remote, independent system of stars.

Gravity is the force of attraction exerted by all bodies in the universe (universal gravitation).

Interstellar All space outside the solar system among the stars.

Light year The distance that light travels in one year (= 9,500,000,000,000 km or 6,000,000,000,000 miles).

Magnitude refers to the brightness of a celestial body.

Meteor A meteor is a flash or streak of light in the night sky caused by a tiny grain of cosmic matter entering the Earth's atmosphere and completely burning up.

Meteorite A body larger and brighter than a meteor which reaches the surface of the Earth partly intact. Most meteorites are stone and metal fragments from broken asteroids.

Moon Another name for satellite (see below).

Nebula (plural nebulae) refers to the cloud-like appearance of a certain kind of celestial body. Because distant galaxies appear cloud-like, they are also loosely termed as 'nebulae', but true nebulae are collections of gas and dust lying inside our own Milky Way.

Newton's laws Isaac Newton, using Kepler's three laws as a starting-point, discovered three more laws that showed how the force of gravity (universal gravitation) kept the planets and comets in orbit round the Sun.

Node A term referring to two points in the Moon's orbit where it crosses the ecliptic (see above). Only when the Moon is on or near the node points can eclipses of the Sun occur.

Nova The name given to an exploding star that has previously been shining much more faintly. When it explodes it becomes much brighter and more noticeable – hence the name **nova**, Latin for 'new'.

Orbit The path of a celestial body moving round another. For example, the Earth moves round the Sun in an orbit taking 365¼ days.

Penumbra The partial shadow as opposed to the full shadow (umbra, see below) which occurs at the time of a partial eclipse of the Sun. Also used to describe the less dark outer parts of Sunspots.

Planet A dark solid body such as the Earth which revolves round the Sun.

Pulsar A new variety of fast-spinning star discovered by radio telescopes in 1967. Pulsars emit signals in pulses, or flashes, with clock-work regularity and are old, dense stars which have burnt up almost all their nuclear fuel.

Quasar, or quasi-stellar object. An unusual kind of celestial body, discovered in the early 1960s, which emits large amounts of energy. Astronomers believe quasars lie at very remote distances from Earth.

Red giant A large type of star which shines in orange-reddish light. For example, Betelgeuse whose diameter is about 400 times larger than the Sun's.

Refraction The Earth's atmosphere acts like a crude lens and bends (or refracts) light rays. Refraction is greatest near the horizon where light rays from outside have a greater thickness of atmosphere to travel through.

Revolution When a body moves in orbit round the Sun, it is said to revolve round it. The Earth has a revolution period round the Sun of 365¼ days.

Rotation When a body spins on its axis, it is said to rotate. The Earth rotates in about 24 hours.

Satellite A name given to a lesser body revolving round a larger one. For example, the Moon is a satellite of the Earth.

Solar cycle The name given to the 11-year period of sunspot activity.

Solar system The family of planets and comets which revolve in orbit round the Sun and are held there by the Sun's gravitational attraction.

Solar wind The name given to radiation particles shot out into space by activity on the Sun.

Spectroscope An instrument attached to a telescope used by astronomers to produce a spectrum of a celestial body.

Spectrum When white light is passed through a glass prism, it is divided into various rainbow colours – to form a spectrum. Much information about the chemical make-up of a celestial body can be found by the examination of its spectrum.

Star A globe of very hot gas like the Sun (Sol) which is a very typical star.

Sun see Star above.

Sunspots are dark, spotty markings on the Sun's surface usually with a dark, umbral, region surrounded by a lighter, penumbral, region.

Supernova An exploding star similar to a nova (see above) but which is an even more spectacular object.

Umbra The name given to the black shadow caused by the Moon at time of total eclipse of the Sun. It is also used to describe the black, central part of a sunspot.

Universe The place in which we live – including the solar system, the Milky Way and all other distant galaxies; sometimes called the cosmos.

Variable star A type of star that varies in brightness (magnitude).

White dwarf A star of high temperature and density but of small diameter. Some white dwarfs are now bigger than the Earth but are millions of times more dense.

Acknowledgments
BBC Hulton Picture Library, Paul Brierley, Camera Press, Hale Observatories, Michael Holford, Archivio IGDA Peter Lancaster Brown, Mansell Collection, Mt Wilson and Palomar Observatories, Ann Ronan Picture Library, Royal Astronomical Society, Science Museum London, Ronald Sheridan Photo Library, Spectrum Colour Library, US Naval Observatory.